Mainstreaming

Mainstreaming

A Special Interest Resource Guide in Education

Compiled by Sara Lake

ORYX PRESS

The rare Arabian Oryx, a desert antelope dating from Biblical times, is believed to be the prototype of the mythical unicorn. The World Wildlife Fund found three of the animals in 1962, and aware that they were nearing extinction, sent them to the Phoenix Zoo as the nucleus of a breeding herd in captivity. Today the Oryx population is nearing 200 and herds have been returned to breeding grounds in Israel and Jordan.

Copyright © 1980 by The Oryx Press
2214 North Central at Encanto
Phoenix, AZ 85004

Published Simultaneously in Canada

Printed and Bound in the United States of America

The abstracts indicated throughout this Resource Guide by an asterisk after the title are published with permission of University Microfilms International, publishers of *Dissertation Abstracts International* (copyright © 1980 by University Microfilms International), and may not be reproduced without their prior permission.

The abstracts indicated throughout this Resource Guide by a dagger after the title are reprinted from *Exceptional Child Education Resources* by permission of The Council for Exceptional Children. Copyright © 1980 by the Council for Exceptional Children.

Library of Congress Cataloging in Publication Data

Lake, Sara.
    Mainstreaming, a special interest resource guide.

    Includes index.
    1. Handicapped children—Education—United States—Addresses, essays, lectures.   2. Main-streaming in education—United States—Addresses, essays, lectures.   I. Title.
LC4031.L32   371.9'046'0973   80-20919
ISBN 0-912700-73-4

Contents

Introduction   vii

Mainstreaming: Philosophy and Law   1
The Education for All Handicapped Children Act of 1975—P.L. 94 142 and Section 504 of the
Rehabilitation Act of 1973   3

Reactions from the Field   9
The Status of Mainstreaming   11

Implementing Mainstreaming: Barriers and Needed Change   21
Attitudes: Acceptance of the Handicapped   23
Roles and Skills   29
New Role Definitions and Training Needs   29
Training Methods and Materials   34
Organizational Change and Program Alternatives   39
Student Placement: Determining the Least Restrictive Environment   51

Making Mainstreaming Work   57
Handbooks, Guidelines, and Resources   59

Index   77

Introduction

Mainstreaming—the placement of handicapped students in regular classrooms—is not synonymous with the Education for All Handicapped Children Act of 1975 (P.L. 94-142), whose "Least Restrictive Environment" provision calls for regular class placement only if that is determined to be the optimal setting for a particular child. Yet the concept of mainstreaming and this law are closely intertwined in current educational thought. Together with federal requirements for architectural accessibility for the disabled (Section 504 of the Rehabilitation Act of 1973) they mandate a new goal for the handicapped—the fullest possible opportunity for integration into the mainstream of school life.

As could be expected in response to a mandate of such scope, mainstreaming has generated a voluminous amount of educational literature. This Resource Guide presents a survey of the most recent published materials (1977 through February, 1980) on the mainstreaming concept and its two related federal laws. The materials presented are about and for school personnel, preschool through university, and parents of the handicapped, who play an important role in meeting the educational needs of their children.

The first section of this guide covers the rationale behind mainstreaming and the provisions of P.L. 94-142 and Section 504. Section two consists mainly of surveys indicating how schools have reacted to the mandate, what has been accomplished, and what problems have been encountered. Mainstreaming requires substantial changes in people's attitudes and roles, in the structure of educational offerings and methods, and in the ways that placement decisions for each child are made. Section three presents each of these issues separately, addressing what changes are needed, what barriers to change exist, and what alternatives and change strategies are possible. Finally, section four presents guidelines on mainstreaming for school personnel and resource lists for further exploration of this issue.

Because the literature is multifaceted, no simple section arrangement could delineate all areas of interest. For this reason, a subject index is provided as an aid to pinpointing citations on more specific questions.

The citations in this guide were compiled from computer searches of nine databases: ERIC; Exceptional Child Education Resources (from the Council for Exceptional Children); Compr[ehensive] [In]dex; Public Affairs Informatio[n Service]; [Psych]ological Abstracts; Sociological Abstrac[ts]; [So]cial SciSearch; Magazine Index; and the National Information Center for Special Education Materials' NICSEM/NIMIS file; as well as from manual searches of Education Index and the extensive library and information files of the San Mateo Educational Resources Center (SMERC).

Within each section or subsection, citations are arranged by document format: journal articles, microfiche documents, and books. Notation is made on those citations known to be available for purchase from a standard source. On selected journal articles, an order number prefaced with the letters "EJ" plus the notation "Reprint: UMI" indicates that a photocopy of the article may be purchased from:

> Article Copy Service-CIJE
> University Microfilms
> International
> 300 North Zeeb Road
> Ann Arbor, Michigan 48106
> (800) 521-3042

All cited microfiche documents have order codes and source acronyms, indicating their availability from one of three ordering sources, as listed below:

DC	University Microfilms Dissertation Copies P.O. Box 1764 Ann Arbor, Michigan 48106 (800) 521-3042
EDRS	ERIC Document Reproduction Service P.O. Box 190 Arlington, Virginia 22210 (703) 841-1212
SMERC	San Mateo Educational Resources Center 333 Main Street Redwood City, California 94063 (415) 364-5600 ext. 4403

MAINSTREAMING:
PHILOSOPHY AND LAW

The Education for All Handicapped Children Act of 1975—P.L. 94–142 and Section 504 of the Rehabilitation Act of 1973

JOURNAL ARTICLES

1. Another Look at Mainstreaming: Exceptionality, Normality, and the Nature of Difference. Sapon-Shevin, Mara. *Phi Delta Kappan*. v60, n2, p119–21, Oct 1978 (EJ 188 651; Reprint: UMI).

Mainstreaming must be conceived of, not as changing the special child so that he will fit back into the unchanged regular classroom, bur rather as changing the nature of the regular classroom so that it is more accommodating to all children.

2. Due Process and Least Restrictive Alternative: New Emphasis on Parental Participation. Chiba, Constance; Semmel, Melvyn I. *Viewpoints*. v53, n2, p17–29, Mar 1977.

This article provides information on the legal principles of due process and least restrictive alternatives, cites pertinent litigation involving these principles in education, and discusses some important educational implications of Public Law 94-142.

3. Due Process and the Handicapped Child. Bateman, Barbara. *Early Years*. v9, n8, p40–42, Apr 1979 (available from Allen Raymond, Inc., P.O. Box 1223, Darien, CT 06820).

The author, a lawyer and a professor of special education, discusses the requirement of "fundamental fairness," minimum and maximum due process, safeguards in special education, and the least restrictive environment concept.

4. The Education for All Handicapped Children Act of 1975. National Perspectives and Long Range Implications. Semmel, Melvyn I.; Heinmiller, Joseph L. *Viewpoints*. v53, n2, p1–16, Mar 1977.

The authors review the legislative antecedents of the Education for All Handicapped Children Act, 1975 (P.L. 94-142), give an overview of the purpose and intent of Congress in enacting the legislation, and discuss some long-range implications for society of the federal role in education.

5. The Handicap Mandate. Woodward, Robert E. *American School and University*. v50, n1, p35–36, 38, 40, Sep 1977 (EJ 165 853; Reprint: UMI).

Key provisions of the Section 504 regulations, and what they mean for school administrators.

6. Least Restrictive Alternative: An Educational Analysis. Klein, Nancy K. *Education and Training of the Mentally Retarded*. v13, n1, p102–14, Feb 1978.

Presented is an educational analysis of the term "least restrictive alternative," with emphasis placed on historical perspectives, a definition of the term, a framework for analyzing elements of the concept, and a set of guiding principles for planning and implementing the concepts.

7. Mainstreaming: The Genesis of an Idea. Kavale, Kenneth. *Exceptional Child*. v26, n1, p3–21, Mar 1979.

Problems of definition are discussed and followed by a delineation of three major forces which induced the genesis of mainstreaming: research-based evidence and arguments, litigation challenging long-established practice, and legislative mandates (specifically, the Education for All Handicapped Children Act— P.L. 94-142).

8. Mainstreaming: Implementing the Spirit of the Law. Sapon-Shevin, Mara. *Journal of Negro Education*. v48, n3, p364–81, Sum 1979 (EJ 210 331; Reprint: UMI).

Traces the direction which the mainstreaming movement has taken to date, analyzes models for organizing schools to best meet the needs of all children, discusses ways for facilitating appropriate changes, and describes the interrelationship between the mainstreaming movement and the desegregation and multicultural education movements.

9. Mainstreaming: Valuing Diversity in Children. Dunlop, Kathleen H. *Young Children*. v32, n4, p26–32, May 1977.

Comments on the growth of mainstreaming, research on placement of special children, and characteristics of a successfully mainstreamed classroom.

10. Mainstreaming for Every Child. Garrett, John Patrick. *Clearing House*. v51, n6, p294–96, Feb 1978 (EJ 180 782; Reprint: UMI).

Discusses the advantages of mainstreaming — combining as many handicapped children into the regular classroom as is possible—and the tragedy of separating those who are marginally handicapped into special education classrooms.

11. **Mainstreaming Mentally Retarded Students in the Public Schools.** Payne, James S. et al. *Mental Retardation*. v17, n1, p45–46, Feb 1979.

The position statement of the National Association for Retarded Citizens regarding the mainstreaming of mentally retarded students is presented.

12. **P.L. 94-142: Answers to the Questions You're Asking.** *Instruction*. v87, n9, p63–65, 72–73, Apr 1978 (EJ 176 181; Reprint: UMI).

Presents questions and answers on the Education for All Handicapped Children Act of 1975, including what it is, what it says, how it helps the handicapped, and how it affects teachers.

13. **The Past and Future Impact of Court Decisions in Special Education.** Turnbull, H. Rutherford, III. *Phi Delta Kappan*. v59, n8, p523–27, Apr 1978 (EJ 175 640; Reprint: UMI).

Reviews the decisions that have established the five principles of special educational law (zero reject, nondiscriminatory evaluation, appropriate education, least restrictive placement, and procedural due process), demonstrates how they have affected federal legislation, and suggests future litigation the courts will face in these areas.

14. **Political and Moral Contexts That Produced P.L. 94-142.** Corrigan, Dean C. *Journal of Teacher Education*. v29, n6, p10–14, Nov–Dec 1978 (EJ 193 337; Reprint: UMI).

The Education for All Handicapped Children Act calls for social, political, and economic reforms, as well as educational reforms.

15. **Public Law 94-142 and Section 504: What They Say about Rights and Protections.** Ballard, Joseph; Zettel, Jeffrey. *Exceptional Children*. v44, n3, p177–84, Nov 1977.

Explained are the basic thrust, objectives, and target populations, as well as the rights and protections provided for in the Education for All Handicapped Children Act (Public Law 94-142) and Section 504 of the Vocational Rehabilitation Act of 1973.

16. **Public Law 94-142 and the Education of Preschool Handicapped Children.** Cohen, Shirley et al. *Exceptional Children*. v45, n4, p279–85, Jan 1979.

From a legal perspective, this article discusses the effect of the Education for All Handicapped Children Act (P.L. 94-142) on the education of preschool handicapped children.

17. **Special Education: Implementation of New Rules.** Klein, Nancy K. *Theory into Practice*. v17, n4, p348–60, Oct 1978 (EJ 198 799; Reprint: UMI).

Topics discussed here include definitions of exceptional persons; the rationale of mainstreaming; racial discrimination in special education placement; law, policy, and court litigation; federal and state legislation and state plan requirements; funding special education; and regional resource centers.

18. **Understanding the "Legal Technicalities" of Federal Regulations.** Guthrie, R. Claire. *New Directions for Higher Education; No. 25 (Assuring Access for the Handicapped)*. v7, n1, p69–79, 1979 (EJ 205 017; Reprint: UMI).

Answers to questions about institutional obligations under Sections 503 and 504 of the Rehabilitation Act of 1973 illustrate the legal issues that may confront college administrators as they make efforts to comply. Topics include: institutions that are covered, individuals who are protected, reasonable accommodation, affirmative action, and legal defenses.

REPORTS

19. **The Concept of Least Restrictive Environment: Implications for Implementation.** * Mittendorf, William Edwin, Ball State University, 1978, 69p (7821108; Reprint: DC).

A documentary research procedure was used to accomplish the purposes of the study. A review of federal legislation and related literature was made to trace the historical development of least restrictive environment. A review and analysis of federal legislation, court decisions, and related literature were made to identify the considerations which must guide school officials to insure that handicapped children will be provided fair and appropriate placement to receive educational programs and services in a setting consistent with and supportive of the concept of least restrictive environment.

The earliest federal legislation providing educational and maintenance care for handicapped persons was passed in 1827. Federal legislation passed during the period from 1827 to 1965 reflected the then current social philosophy that handicapped individuals should be segregated from the general public and be served in separate "asylums." Federal legislation designed to mandate educational and/or maintenance care for handicapped persons passed during the period from 1967 through 1975 has reflected the developing philosophy that handicapped persons have the same civil and human rights as nonhandicapped persons, particularly as such rights relate to educational programs and services.

The concept of "least restrictive environment," as described by law, means that handicapped children must be educated in the most normal setting feasible; must be educated, to the maximum extent appropriate, with nonhandicapped students; must be given access and opportunity to participate in nonacademic and extracurricular activities; and regular and special education programs must be physically accessible to handicapped students.

Findings of the study show that handicapped students have the same legal right to a free, tax-supported education as do nonhandicapped students. When considering educational programs and services to be provided for handicapped children, the basic assumption must be that the child can best be accommodated in a regular classroom setting. If and as school officials secure hard evidence that a handicapped child cannot be served adequately in a regular classroom setting, special programs and support services, as may be appropriate, must be developed for the student. Public school officials have a legal obligation to provide whatever specialized instruction is required for the child. A lack of funds does not relieve school officials from the obligation to provide needed special education. When considering any change of placement for a child, due process procedures must be followed. Educational programs and services given must be designed to help the handicapped student develop behavioral patterns acceptable in the community. Therefore, special education programs and services should be organized in such a way as to provide extensive opportunities to interact with the community. Entrance requirements, such as standardized tests, which discriminate against handicapped students, may not be used to determine eligibility for participation in a specific program unless school officials can demonstrate that the entrance requirement is necessary to successful completion of the specific program.

It is clear that, even though federal legislation has mandated educational programs for handicapped children, the judicial branch of government has provided the directives and guidelines which have resulted in the implementation of programs for the handicapped.

The concept of least restrictive environment is as much a philosophical attitude as it is a legal definition. The least restrictive environment involves an emotional as well as a physical acceptance of handicapped students into a particular building or classroom.

20. Concordance for the Implementation of P.L. 94-142.
Ameruoso, Frank A., Allegheny Intermediate Unit, Pittsburgh, PA, 1978, 259p; print is marginal and may not reproduce well in hard copy. Sponsoring agency: Bureau of Education for the Handicapped (DHEW/OE), Washington, DC (ED 155 847; Reprint: EDRS).

The concordance is designed to serve as a reference for administrators, supervisors, and others responsible for the implementation of P.L. 94-142, Education for All Handicapped Children Act. Specific references to the law along with compliance policy and procedure guidelines are presented in table format for the following major divisions of the federal regulations: administration; advisory panel (state); allocations; annual program plan; applicability of regulations; application by a local agency; complaints; comparable services; consent; confidentiality of information; count of children; due process; evaluation; excess costs; free appropriate public education; full educational opportunity goal; handicapped children; hearings; identification, location, and evaluation; Indian children; individualized education program; least restrictive environment; matching (state funds); monitoring; nondiscrimination; notice; personnel development; physical education; priorities; private school children; procedural safeguards; public participation; records; related services; reports; special education; state advisory panel; state direct and support services; supplanting (with federal funds); surrogate parents; time limits and timetables; and use of Part B funds.

21. The Education for All Handicapped Children Act (P.L. 94-142): Preserving Both Children's and Teachers' Rights.
Rauth, Marilyn, American Federation of Teachers, Washington, DC, 1978, 12p (ED 162 979; Reprint: EDRS; also available from American Federation of Teachers, AFL-CIO, 11 Dupont Circle, NW, Washington, DC 20036).

Common problems and questions raised in implementation of P.L. 94-142 are dealt with in this pamphlet. The purpose of this publication is to help teachers and other school employees use the law to protect the interests of all children and their own rights as professionals. The following areas of concern are discussed in question-answer format: (1) basic requirements; (2) individualized education programs (IEPs); (3) less restrictive environment placements; (4) due process; (5) state and local regulations; and (6) noncompliance.

22. Mainstreaming: Merging Regular and Special Education.
Hasazi, Susan E. et al., Phi Delta Kappa Educational Foundation, Bloomington, IN, 1979, 48p (ED 175 212; Reprint: EDRS; also available from Phi Delta Kappa Educational Foundation, 8th Street and Union Avenue, Bloomington, IN 47401).

The booklet on mainstreaming looks at the merging of special and regular education as a process rather than as an end. Chapters address the following topics (sample subtopics in parentheses): what is mainstreaming; pros and cons of mainstreaming; forces influencing change in special education (educators, parents and advocacy groups, the courts, federal policy, and legislation); the intent of P.L. 94-142, the Education for All Handicapped Children Act (state requirements, local education agency requirements, zero reject model of education, individualized educational program, least restrictive environment, nondiscriminatory testing, and due process safeguards); roles and responsibilities of regular and special educators parent-teacher partnership (professional mishandling of parents and parents' mishandling of professionals); implications for the future (research); and gaining community support.

23. Mainstreaming (Part 1).
Pittsburgh Area Preschool Association, PA, Jan 1978, 28p (ED 153 381; Reprint: EDRS; also available from Children in Contemporary Society, P.O. Box 11173, Pittsburgh, PA 15237).

The first of two issues devoted to an analysis of mainstreaming for handicapped students includes eight papers on aspects of the topic. Papers consider public awareness and acceptance of the handicapped; implications of Section 504 (Vocational Rehabilitation Act of 1973); components of P.L. 94-142, the Education for All Handicapped Children Act; identification, assessment, placement, and accountability issues related to P.L. 94-142; student records and the Family Educational Rights and Privacy Act; effects of mainstreaming on nonhandicapped young children; and the impact of mainstreaming on parents.

24. Mainstreaming (Part 2).
Pittsburgh Area Preschool Association, PA, Mar 1978, 26p (ED 153 382; Reprint: EDRS; also available from Children in Contemporary Society, P.O. Box 11173, Pittsburgh, PA 15237).

The second of two issues addresses topics related to mainstreaming of handicapped children. Considered in nine articles are the following topics: the administrator's role; legal issues involved in the least restrictive environment specification of P.L. 94-142, the Education For All Handicapped Children Act; parents' and teachers' views regarding mainstreaming; a summary of research; a review of professional literature and resources on mainstreaming; and a description of six children's books concerning handicapped children.

25. Mainstreaming: Problems, Potentials, and Perspectives. Bates, Percy, Ed. et al., Michigan University, Ann Arbor, School of Education, 1977, 128p. Sponsoring agency: Bureau of Education for the Handicapped (DHEW/OE), Washington, DC, Division of Personnel Preparation (ED 163 671; Reprint: EDRS; also limited copies of these papers are available from the National Support Systems Project, 253 Burton Hall, 173 Pillsbury Drive, SE, Minneapolis, MN 55455).

The book presents a series of papers on mainstreaming that were part of a University of Michigan seminar for special education doctoral students. In Part I, "The Origins and Evolution of Mainstreaming," the authors discuss the various forces that have encouraged the development of mainstreaming and the least-restrictive-environment concept, including the historical emergence of special education as a field, American attitudes toward the handicapped, litigative and legislative factors in mainstreaming, the Education of All Handicapped Children Act (P.L. 94-142), and parents. Part II, "The Implications of Mainstreaming," focuses on four important areas: the sources of resistance to the inclusion of special needs children in regular classrooms, several critical issues raised by mainstreaming for the public schools, mainstreaming's implications for non-White children, and teacher training for mainstreaming.

26. Mainstreaming across Nations. Hansen, Philip A.; Hansen, Shirley B. Jan 1979, 13p; Paper presented at the Annual Meeting of the Claremont Reading Conference (46th, Claremont, CA, January 19–20, 1979) (ED 167 985; Reprint: EDRS).

An overview of mainstreaming in various nations is presented in this paper. Following a discussion of the background of mainstreaming, the paper offers brief analyses of mainstreaming trends in the United States; the Nordic countries; the nine Common Market nations; and the socialist countries, specifically the Soviet Union. The paper concludes that mainstreaming is a worldwide phenomenon, that no nation has devised the ultimate plan for mainstreaming, that the key to successful mainstreaming is the regular classroom teacher, and that it is time for educators in the United States to implement the provisions of Public Law 94-142, written to integrate exceptional individuals.

27. P.L. 94-142 "Not Just a Law — A Darn Good Idea" A Resource Packet for Use in the Conference: Advancing the Handicapped and School Administration. Drake University, Des Moines, IA, Midwest Regional Resource Center, 1977, 163p. Sponsoring agency: American Association of School Administrators, Washington, DC; Bureau of Education for the Handicapped (DHEW/OE), Washington, DC (ED 161 188; Reprint: EDRS).

Presented is a resource packet used in a conference designed to create and develop a greater awareness and understanding of the implications of the Education for All Handicapped Children Act (P.L. 94-142). The packet is divided into six sections. The first section deals with P.L. 94-142 and provides an overview of the law, a compliance matrix, definitions of terms, and full service planning forms. Section 2 focuses on individualized education programs and includes selected regulations for P.L. 94-142 and an analysis worksheet. Procedural safeguards are covered in section 3; provided

are questions and answers regarding due process and record-keeping and confidentiality, a self-administered due process guide, policy regarding nondiscriminatory evaluation, and policies for the development and use of anecdotal records. Section 4 identifies some of the possible resources in the area of personnel development. The fifth section presents 12 programs known as operationalizing the least restrictive environment. The last section alphabetically lists 42 resources.

28. Public Law 94-142: The Education for All Handicapped Children Act. An Overview of the Federal Law. Zettel, Jeffrey J. Mar 1977, 13p; Paper presented at the Annual Meeting of the Association for Supervision and Curriculum Development (32nd, Houston, TX, March 19–23, 1977) (ED 140 554; Reprint: EDRS).

Provided is an overview of the Education for all Handicapped Children Act (Public Law 94-142), including a report of the history of federal involvement in the education of the handicapped. Sections cover ten critical issues dealt with in the new law, such as the concepts of zero reject, appropriate education, and least restrictive alternative, and provisions for procedural safeguards, single agency responsibility, training of professional personnel, and accountability. In summary, it is noted that the following are the specific purposes of the law: (1) to insure publicly funded special education and related services for all handicapped children no later than 1978; (2) to insure the rights of handicapped children and their parents and guardians; (3) to relieve the special education financial burden of state and local governments; and (4) to assess and insure the effectiveness of efforts to educate handicapped children.

29. Public Law 94-142: Special Education in Transition. Barbacovi, Don R.; Clelland, Richard W., American Association of School Administrators, Arlington, VA, 1978, 91p (ED 172 412; Reprint: EDRS; also available from American Association of School Administrators, 1801 North Moore Street, Arlington, VA 22209).

The purpose of this handbook is to examine the statutory and regulatory requirements of Public Law 94-142, the Education for All Handicapped Children Act, and to outline various administrative responsibilities of local educational agencies relative to the successful implementation of the act. Four specific goals are listed: (1) to inform public school administrators of the statutory and regulatory requirements of the act, (2) to identify critical issues and describe possible problem areas, (3) to describe the effect that the act could have on organizational structure and operations, and (4) to examine the effect that the act could have on administrative decision making and evaluation of criteria for program effectiveness. Divided into seven chapters, the book discusses some of the following: the history of P.L. 94-142, local educational agency applications for federal funds, the least restrictive environment in which to educate the handicapped, procedural due process requirements, the requirement for individualized education programs, and personnel development requirements. The book concludes that all segments of society, not just the public schools, must change to accommodate the handicapped.

30. A Teacher's Reference Guide to PL 94-142. INFOPAC No. 11. National Education Association, Washington, DC, Division of Instruction and Professional Development, 1978, 56p (ED 156 663; Reprint: EDRS-HC not available; also available from National Education Association Distribution Center, The Academic Building, West Haven, CT 06516).

Major provisions of Public Law 94-142, the Education for All Handicapped Children Act, are cited and discussed in this guide for teacher association leaders and staff. The role of local and state educational agencies in providing a free, appropriate, public education for handicapped students and methods for involving teachers, their associations, and parents in this effort are investigated. Relevant passages from Section 504 of the Rehabilitation Act of 1973 (a civil rights law addressing, among others, the topic of education) and of P.L. 94-142, as well as supporting regulations for each of the acts, are highlighted. The document is divided into four sections devoted to: (1) general provisions of P.L. 94-142, purpose, definition of terms, priorities, relationship between P.L. 94-142 and Section 504; (2) providing a free, appropriate, public education for handicapped children, preplacement evaluation, evaluation timeliness, individualized education programs (IEPs), placement in least restrictive environments, teacher appeals of placement, physical education for the handicapped, learning materials, school district liability for educational services; (3) special teacher concerns, class size, personnel, compliance procedures, student attitudes, elimination of physical barriers, coordination of regular and special education programs, inservice education, teacher association involvement; (4) rights of parents of handicapped, children-parent participation in the IEP, independent evaluation, parental consent and notification, confidentiality of information, and procedural due process rights of parents.

31. A Workable Interpretation of Federal Guidelines for Administering Special Education Programs (PL 94-142). Lovitt, Bebe, Arizona State University, Tempe, Arizona Educational Information System, Bureau of Educational Research and Services, 1978, 93p (ID 005 950; Reprint: SMERC—HC not available).

This resource guide, designed to assist school boards, administrators, teachers, and other school personnel in understanding and preparing for P.L. 94-142, is a comprehensive analysis and review of the "Education for All Handicapped Children Act." In addition to a detailed interpretation of the act, a Compliance Checklist is included as Appendix C.

REACTIONS FROM THE FIELD

The Status of Mainstreaming

JOURNAL ARTICLES

32. Adapting to the Revolution of Equal Opportunity for the Handicapped. Bailey, Cornelia W. *New Directions for Higher Education; No. 25 (Assuring Access for the Handicapped).* v7, n1, p81–111, 1979 (EJ 205 018; Reprint: UMI).

Federal regulations regarding the handicapped pose problems for recipients of federal aid, but higher education's reactions have been more positive than negative. The principle problems seem to be compliance costs, the need for interpretation of the regulations, and difficulties in the areas of admissions and academic requirements.

33. Considerations of the Implementation of PL 94-142 in the State of Georgia. Behrend, Mary W.; Shimkus, James P. *Journal of the International Association of Pupil Personnel Workers.* v22, n4, p204–06, 235, Sep 1978 (EJ 188 412; Reprint: UMI).

Problems in implementing P.L. 94-142, including insufficient funding, lack of trained personnel, accountability, and labeling are discussed. The roles of normal children, parents, and professionals are also considered.

34. Experienced Mainstreamers Speak Out. Yaffe, Elaine. *Teacher.* v96, n6, p61–63, Feb 1979 (EJ 207 587; Reprint: UMI).

Regular class teachers from Colorado Springs, where mainstreaming has been practiced for several years, comment on its advantages and disadvantages, their need for support, and the emotional and professional demands mainstreaming makes on them. Particular attention is given to the difficulties of handling emotionally disturbed children.

35. Fair Hearings Have Big Impact on Local Agencies. Johnson, James E. et al. *Thrust for Educational Leadership.* v9, n2, p17, 24, Nov 1979 (EJ 213 734; Reprint: UMI).

Presented are the results of a survey conducted to determine the impact of state and federal fair hearing mandates on California school districts and county offices of education. The laws governing the selection of fair hearing panels, and the selection process itself are also included.

36. Initial Impact of Federal Special Education Legislation: PL 94-142. *Journal of Education.* v161, n3, p1–89, Sum 1979.

This theme journal issue presents five articles which consider various aspects of the history and provisions of the Education for All Handicapped Children Act (P.L. 94-142) and reactions to it from the field. Articles are: "The Education for All Handicapped Children Act of 1975: Its History, Origins, and Concepts," "Can Old Dogs be Taught New Tricks or Will SEA Directors Be Allowed to Monitor?," "Procedural Due Process: The Two-Edged Sword That the Untrained Should Not Unsheath," "P.L. 94-142 and the Least Restrictive Alternative: An Interim Progress Report for Educators," and "The Impact of PL 94-142 at the LEA Level."

37. Mainstreaming: Time for Reassessment. Linton, Thomas E.; Juul, Kristen D. *Educational Leadership.* v37, n5, p433–37, Feb 1980.

The authors analyze four basic assumptions behind the mainstreaming movement, pointing out that the issues are far more complex than they might appear. Citing mainstreaming experiences in other countries, especially Scandinavia, they emphasize the need for careful planning and for new organizational alternatives.

38. Mainstreaming in Perspective. Brooks, Andree. *Teacher.* v96, n8, p58–59, Apr 1979 (EJ 218 901, Reprint: UMI).

Teachers associations are discovering a grass roots reaction of concern, frustration, and resentment surfacing among regular classroom teachers over the way they say administrators are implementing P.L. 94-142. However, some help for teachers is on the way, through inservice training and new weighted class size formulas.

39. Notice and Consent: The School's Responsibility to Inform Parents. Hoff, Maryann K. et al. *Journal of School Psychology.* v16, n3, p265–73, Fall 1978 (EJ 188 397; Reprint: UMI).

Parental involvement in planning and placement for 20 children initially referred for special education is described in light of the P.L. 94-142 requirements for informed parental consent. Comparisons indicate that parents' versions of each decision component were clear and accurate no more than 50 percent of the time, even though parents were present at the team meetings where these decisions were rendered.

40. Progress in Mainstreaming. Wendel, Frederick C. *Phi Delta Kappan*. v59, n1, p58, Sep 1977 (EJ 164 220; Reprint: UMI).

According to the respondents (state department of education personnel), mainstreaming activities have progressed significantly since 1971, with only a relative minority, roughly one-fifth, of the districts lagging behind the others.

41. Rarely Have So Many Done So Much with So Little, Study Says of P.L. 94–142. (Education for All Handicapped Children Act.) *Phi Delta Kappan*. v60, n7, p544, Mar 1979.

State and local education agencies have worked aggressively to carry out provisions of the Education for All Handicapped Children Act, Public Law 94-142, even though the federal government contributed only 5 percent of the extra costs of special education, according to Education Turnkey Systems. The Washington-based firm studied performance of three state and nine local education agencies under P.L. 94-142. Its report noted that, when compared with activity initiated under other recent legislation, a great deal has been accomplished under the handicapped children act.

42. Responses to P.L. 94-142: Institutional Changes for Preservice Teacher Preparation. Butler, Michael J. *Journal of Teacher Education*. v29, n6, p77–79, Nov-Dec 1978 (EJ 193 354; Reprint: UMI).

The response of teacher educators and teacher education institutions to the demands of the Education for All Handicapped Children Act is discussed.

43. Teacher Education and Mainstreaming: A Status Report for the South. Roberson, Julius B. *Phi Delta Kappan*. v61, n1, p70, Sep 1979.

Reports a survey of teacher education institutions in the Southern Association of Colleges and Schools on the status of their plans for faculty inservice and curricular modifications to prepare teachers for mainstreaming.

44. Update on Education of the Handicapped. Massie, Dorothy. *Today's Education*. v67, n3, p60–62, 73, Sep-Oct 1978 (EJ 198 775; Reprint: UMI).

Problems faced by teachers and schools in educating handicapped students are described, and recommendations for improving the situation are offered. This article is based on the report of the NEA Study Panel on Education of Handicapped Children.

45. Working with the IEP: Some Early Reports. Hawkins-Shepard, Charlotte. *Teaching Exceptional Children*. v10, n3, p95–97, Spr 1978.

Interviews with 11 teachers, specialists, and administrators focus on development of individualized education programs (IEPs) for handicapped students. Noted are positive changes which are occurring and areas where further change is needed.

REPORTS

46. An Analysis of Rural and Urban Elementary Schools in Alabama to Determine Their Architectural Accessibility to Handicapped Students.* Overstreet, Susan Manly McMillan, The University of Alabama, 1978, 296p (7905425; Reprint: DC).

The purpose of this study was to analyze elementary schools in randomly selected rural and urban school systems in Alabama to determine their current degree of compliance with the specific barrier free architectural criteria described in Section 504 of Public Law 93-112, and Public Law 94-142, the Education for All Handicapped Children Act.

A statistically determined sample of 67 elementary facilities was selected by use of a random numbers table. Thirty-nine of these schools were rural and 28 were urban. Upon receiving written permission from the superintendents, on-site visits were made to these facilities over a three month period by a single reviewer, and the data recorded on the Facility Accessibility Checklist forms. Data were key punched and processed by computer.

Chi square analyses of the data gathered on the Facility Accessibility Checklists from the 67 elementary schools in the sample indicated no statistically significant difference in overall response between rural and urban schools on the 95 barrier free specification criteria. Of the 95 criteria, only ten were statistically significant. These items fell into the categories of walks, stairs and steps, restrooms, and water fountains. Rural-urban differences on these items were probably due to the presence of more multiple story school buildings, more separate grammar school facilities (as opposed to combined grammar school-high school compounds), and more standardized hardware in urban areas. The above factors (building height, separate elementary facilities, and standardized hardware) along with other general characteristics were derived from response to general questions on the fore sheet of the Facility Accessibility Checklist. Literature on barrier free architecture suggested that these elements could effect the degree of compliance of a particular school to barrier free specification criteria.

On-site review of the 67 elementary schools in the sample indicated no apparent relationship between extent of compliance to barrier free criteria and the presence, type, and age of special education programs; nor was there relationship between compliance and the number of physically handicapped students in a particular school.

Of the 67 elementary schools in the sample, 52 schools belonged to systems actively engaged in programs to identify and eliminate architectural barriers. Fifteen schools (all of them rural) belonged to systems not yet actively engaged in a systemwide program toward compliance with the barrier free requirements of Public Law 94-142.

In summary, this study revealed no statistical difference in overall percent of compliance to barrier free architectural criteria between rural and urban elementary schools in Alabama. Despite the 1978 deadline for meeting barrier free criteria specified in Public Law 94-142, few elementary facilities were found to be totally compliant at this date.

47. Case Study of the Implementation of P.L. 94-142: Preliminary Findings Summary. Education Turnkey Systems, Inc., Washington, DC, Jun 1978, 78p; Contains some small print (ED 172 470; Reprint: EDRS).

The paper discusses the activities and processes by which the local education agencies (LEAs) are implementing the provisions of Public Law 94-142 (Education for All Handicapped Children Act) and describes and analyzes the consequences which occur at the individual LEA/community level. The preliminary findings of a series of nine case studies of LEAs in rural, suburban, and urban settings in three states are presented. After reporting the general findings, the paper explores the activities and consequences of the major provisions of the law (childfind efforts, individualized educational plans, evaluation, placement, due process and parent involvement, and least restrictive environment). Processes and consequences common to all states and those unique to one setting are related. The process dynamics of implementation at the LEA level are explored. Appendixes include State Education Agency and LEA descriptive information, summary descriptions of the case studies, activities and study methodology, and summary tables of the consequences.

48. A Comparison between the Perceived Concerns of Elementary School Principals and Teachers toward Mainstreaming.* Bosman, Robert Garrott, Northern Illinois University, 1979, 185p (7924369; Reprint: DC).

The basic research problem was to ascertain the relationship between the concerns of the elementary school principal administering the innovation, "mainstreaming," and the concerns of teachers involved in teaching in the mainstreaming program. The total participation in the study consisted of 76 elementary school principals and 817 elementary school teachers in the northern Illinois region whose superintendents and/or principals agreed to involve the school district in the study. Principals and teachers from 93 school systems agreed to participate. They were asked to respond to two survey instruments. The first instrument consisted of 18 demographic questions and items. The second instrument, the Stages of Concern Questionnaire, was developed at The Research and Development Center for Teacher Education, The University of Texas at Austin. This latter instrument consisted of 35 statements of concern. The Stages of Concern Questionnaire was a Likert-type instrument which allowed respondents to react to the statements of concern by indicating how closely each statement described a concern they felt at that point in time.

The findings and conclusions generated from the research study were analyzed and the major conclusions were as follows:

1. Elementary school principals' concerns toward mainstreaming were typical of non-users of an innovation.

2. Elementary school teachers' concerns toward mainstreaming were typical of non-users of an innovation.

3. Elementary school principals were more concerned about the impact of mainstreaming on students and colleagues than on themselves.

4. Elementary school teachers were more concerned with the effect of mainstreaming on themselves than with the impact on others.

5. There was no clear pattern of how demographic characteristics of principals affected or related to the Stages of Concern in mainstreaming.

6. More elementary school teachers' concerns were affected by demographic characteristics than were principals' concerns.

7. Teachers with more years of teaching experience tended to be less concerned and negative toward mainstreaming than did teachers with fewer years of teaching experience.

8. Teachers with a background in mainstreaming; that is, formal training, familiarity with Public Law 94-142, use of individualized educational programs (IEPs), and time spent working with mainstreamed children, viewed the concept of mainstreaming more positively than did teachers with no background in mainstreaming by exhibiting low self concerns and higher impact concerns.

49. A Comparison of Concerns of Elementary Teachers, Administrators, and Special Educators toward the Concept of Mainstreaming the Mildly Handicapped in Selected Nebraska Public Schools.* Hartnett, Marjorie Sheahan, The University of Nebraska - Lincoln, 1979, 103p (7920994; Reprint: DC).

The purpose of the study was to analyze and compare the concerns of elementary teachers, administrators, and special education personnel toward the concept of mainstreaming. Specifically, the purpose of this study was to investigate the concerns of these three groups about mainstreaming, and the degree to which these concerns varied among elementary teachers, administrators, and special educators in selected Nebraska schools. Factors which might influence teachers' attitudes toward mainstreaming were identified. Current mainstreaming practices as perceived by elementary teachers, administrators, and special educators were identified.

A review of selected literature was made to determine concerns about mainstreaming and mainstreaming practices. Interviews with educators were conducted to identify their concerns about mainstreaming. Concern statements were formulated from these two sources. An instrument was designed to measure relative intensity of concern pertaining to each statement about mainstreaming. The respondents were also asked to identify current mainstreaming practices in the selected schools.

Data received from the 145 respondents, which included 24 administrators, 27 special educators, and 92 elementary teachers, were tabulated and analyzed regarding their concerns about mainstreaming and the current identifiable mainstreaming practices in their schools. A correlation of the data was calculated using analysis of variance. The .05 level of confidence was set for the determination of significant differences between teachers, administrators, and special educators.

The findings from the study indicated:

1. Elementary teachers and special educators generally tended to be in agreement about mainstreaming concerns. These two groups viewed the concerns as being more serious than did the school administrators.

2. The elementary teachers and the special educators showed a greater concern about meeting the individual needs of all students, both regular and handicapped, than did the school administrators.

3. The need for time to work and plan together was a concern expressed by both the elementary teacher and special educator.

4. Elementary teachers were generally more concerned about student needs, curriculum, and teacher needs than the school administrators.

5. When teacher concerns about mainstreaming were examined, only lack of experience with the handicapped was a significant factor.

6. The elementary teachers who lacked experience with the handicapped student showed a significantly greater concern about mainstreaming than teachers who had had experience with handicapped students.

7. The resource room/resource teacher model was reported as the most commonly found alternative method of providing for the handicapped student.

50. **Comparisons among Principals, Regular Classroom Teachers, and Special Education Teachers of Their Perceptions of the Extent of Implementation of Administrative Practices Pertaining to Mainstreaming Mildly Handicapped Students.** Amos, Neil G.; Moody, Lamar. 1977, 15p (ED 168 241; Reprint: EDRS).

The perceptions of 355 principals, regular classroom teachers, and special education teachers regarding the extent of implementation of administrative practices pertaining to the mainstreaming of mildly handicapped children in Mississippi were studied. The results indicated that the first year of mainstreaming in Mississippi saw only moderate implementation of administrative practices considered essential to effective mainstreaming programs. Analysis identified three areas where the perceptions of the three groups of professionals were not congruent (whether or not the principal should become cognizant of the characteristics of mildly handicapped children, whether or not community resources should be utilized in exceptional child education, and whether or not teachers should be encouraged to educate children about handicaps), thus indicating a need for cooperative planning in developing a rationale for mainstreaming mildly handicapped children in the years ahead.

51. **A Comprehensive Study into the Effects and Changes upon Professional Staff of Montgomery County Intermediate Unit 23 as a Result of IEP Implementation.** Montgomery County Intermediate Unit 23, Blue Bell, PA, Apr 1978, 213p; not available in hard copy due to print quality (ED 166 910; Reprint: EDRS—HC not available).

The report presents results of a survey of Montgomery County (Pennsylvania) Intermediate Unit 23 special education staff (supervisors, master itinerant teachers, teachers, clinicians, therapists, psychologists, social workers, and instructional aids) regarding problems with individualized education programs. Problems and solutions found from open-ended surveys are summarized by 12 program areas: educable mentally retarded, hearing, learning and adjustment, learning disabilities, physically handicapped, severely/profoundly mentally retarded, trainable mentally retarded, gifted, speech, vision, aids, and social workers. Recommendations are made for financial reimbursement or compensatory time benefits for staff to fulfill increasing responsibilities associated with P.L. 94-142, the Education for All Handicapped Children Act. The bulk of the document is composed of appendixes, including a sample survey form, impact sheet form, and edited comments arranged by program.

52. **Educating All the Handicapped: What the Law Says and What the Schools Are Doing.** Savage, David G., National School Public Relations Association, Arlington, VA, 1977, 97p (ED 143 186; Reprint: EDRS—HC not available; also available from National School Public Relations Association, 1801 N. Moore Street, Arlington, VA 22209).

In describing the implications for public schools of P.L. 94-142, the Education for All Handicapped Children Act, the booklet cites reactions of local and state administrators, supervisors, and classroom teachers. The first chapter details the content of P.L. 94-142, provides comments from lawmakers and educators, and lists questions and answers about the law and section 504 of the Rehabilitation Act of 1973. A historical account of the court cases involving educational rights for the handicapped is given. Considered in subsequent chapters are the following topics: the role of state and local education agencies, early intervention, the development of individualized programs, mainstreaming, interpretations of learning disabilities, teacher training, working with parents, and architectural modifications in school facilities.

53. **Education for All Handicapped Children: Consensus, Conflict, and Challenge.** National Education Association, Washington, DC, Teacher Rights Division, 1978, 47p (ED 157 214; Reprint: EDRS—HC not available; also available from National Education Association, 1201 16th Street, NW, Washington, DC 20036).

Presented are the results of a study by the National Education Association of the experience of 43 schools in three selected districts (Des Moines, Iowa; North Santa Barbara County, California; and Savannah, Georgia) in implementing Public Law 94-142 to provide a free, appropriate public education for the handicapped in the least restrictive environment. Positive aspects of the implementation are discussed, along with areas of conflict and labeling. Also discussed are problems in the areas of student testing and evaluation (such as over-referral), educational equity and access (such as weighted enrollment funding), and involvement of parents (such as the need for early parent counseling). Among the recommendations presented are the launching of a program to locate, identify, and evaluate children in need of special education services, and the elimination of group-administered, norm-referenced standardized tests. Appended are a list of steering committees from each study location and a glossary of terms used.

54. **Education of the Handicapped Litigation Brought under P.L. 94-142 and Section 504.** Kowal, Sharon A., George Washington University, Washington, DC, Institute for Educational Leadership, Sep 1978, 21p. Sponsoring agency: Bureau of Education for the Handicapped (DHEW/OE), Washington, DC (ED 162 470; Reprint: EDRS; also available from National Association of State Directors of Special Education, 1201 16th Street, NW, Suite 601 E, Washington, DC 20036 or Education of the Handicapped Policy Project, Institute for Educational Leadership, Suite 310, 1001 Connecticut Avenue, NW, Washington, DC 20036).

The document identifies the legal issues arising from the Education for All Handicapped Children Act (P.L. 94-142) and Section 504 of the Rehabilitation Act of 1973, and indicates how the courts are handling these issues. Annotations on court cases are arranged in major categories; free appropriate public education, placement in the least restrictive environment, placement at no cost to the parent, due process procedures, discipline/expulsion, exhaustion of administrative remedies, miscellaneous cases decided under P.L. 94-142 or Section 504, cases that pose future P.L. 94-142 and Section 504 issues, and cases to note. Within each category the cases are listed chronologically with the most recent case first.

55. The Effect of Collective Negotiations on Mainstreaming Michigan's Special Education Students into Regular Education.* Stewart, Dorothy Louise, Michigan State University, 1978, 193p (7900751; Reprint: DC).

The author's purposes in this study were: (1) to determine to what extent special education students are being mainstreamed into regular education; (2) to determine what types of disabled students are being so integrated; (3) to determine to what extent and what types of contractual provisions address themselves to the mainstreaming of special education students, and (4) to determine what, if any, issues teachers want negotiated in 1977-78 contracts.

The problem to which the researcher in this investigation addressed herself was the problem of the school administrator who faces the dilemma of operating under mandates from the state and federal government requiring that the school district provide for education of the handicapped student within the mainstream of general education and the teachers within the district negotiating to restrict the numbers of handicapped students placed in their classrooms.

The study consisted of three major parts. The first was a survey of fourth Friday count figures of special education students in 142 local school districts and 19 intermediate school districts.

The second survey consisted of searching the 1976-77 negotiated contracts of the same school districts and categorizing the kind and number of items listed in the contracts referring to special education students mainstreamed into regular education.

The third part of the study entailed a telephone survey with the UniServ Directors of the teachers' bargaining units to determine the extent of concern and direction the teachers would be pursuing in regard to mainstreaming in their 1977-78 negotiated contracts.

Twenty-nine findings are reported. The major findings were:
1. Of the 142 local districts studies, 127 reported program for handicapped.
2. Of these 127 local districts and 19 intermediate districts, 2 small districts and 1 intermediate district reported no mainstreaming.
3. EMI, LD, EL, POHI, HI, VI, and TMI students were mainstreamed.
4. While some districts did not mainstream students from all of their basic classroom programs, other districts had handicapped students spending up to 99 percent of their time in general education.
5. One hundred twelve of 135 contracts analyzed had provisions which could affect mainstreaming.
6. Seventy-one contracts had provisions under Protection of Teacher category which related to the removal of the handicapped student from the regular classroom or giving additional help to the teacher with such students.
7. There was much concern on the part of the teachers about mainstreaming.
8. Teachers want concessions made on the part of the administration in the form of more training, materials, and compensatory time for their part in educating the handicapped child.

The following major conclusions were made:
1. The Michigan Department of Education reporting of mainstreaming is inadequate.
2. Most general educators do not feel adequately trained to take on the problems of mainstreaming.
3. If the teachers' wishes, concerns and demands in connection with mainstreaming are going to be met, it will require more resources in the form of money and time, and consequently more general education teachers.

4. Administrators are going to have increased problems because of mainstreaming. They are going to somehow have to help solve what the teachers see as problems caused by it.

56. Evaluation of the Process of Mainstreaming Handicapped Children into Project Head Start. Phase II, Executive Summary. Applied Management Sciences, Inc., Silver Spring, MD, Dec 1978, 24p; Parts marginally legible due to small print. Sponsoring agency: Administration for Children, Youth, and Families (DHEW), Washington, DC (ED 168 291; Reprint: EDRS; Full Report: ED 168 239, 480 p).

The report summarizes the findings and conclusions from the second and final year of an evaluation of Head Start's efforts to serve handicapped children. It is explained that baseline and posttest data were collected on 391 handicapped Head Start students, 321 handicapped children in non-Head Start preschool programs, and 121 unserved handicapped children. Results of comparative analyses are seen to indicate that Ss in both Head Start and non-Head Start programs (particularly speech impaired Ss) showed gains in motoric, self-help, social, academic, and communication skills that were generally greater than those of nonserved Ss. Data also is reported to show that Head Start compared favorably with other service alternatives in terms of child-specific outcomes. Other findings reported include that program benefits for Head Start Ss were variously associated with the amount of time Ss spent in a mainstreaming situation, small class sizes, and low ratios of handicapped to nonhandicapped Ss.

57. A Five-Year Longitudinal Study of IEP Implementation. Turner, Ruth M.; Macy, Daniel J. Feb 1978, 93p; Paper presented at the CEC National Topical Conference on Individualized Education Program Planning (Albuquerque, NM, February, 1978) (ED 170 983; Reprint: EDRS).

The paper describes a five-year longitudinal study of a Texas school district's implementation of an individualized mainstream special education program. "Plan A" program activities and outcomes are reported for five phases (sample subtopics in parentheses): initiation in one high school, one junior high school, and eight elementary schools (description of pilot model and analysis of survey responses and site visits which indicated major implementation difficulties); revision of Pilot Plan A (establishment of an advisory council and materials center); expansion of the pilot program (development of a recordkeeping system for individualized education programs—IEPs, evaluation findings that 60 percent of the plans were complete, and a list of sample objectives for 30 categories); continuation of the pilot program (a teacher workshop for 200 teachers on IEPs and evaluation of student progress which showed that Plan A students made larger gains than expected); and the final phase of district-wide program expansion (the addition of new staff and four format options for IEPs). The report concludes with guidelines for IEP implementation in large urban settings, with 15 common problems pointed out.

58. Handicapped Learner Participation in Vocational Education: A Report on Student, Parent, and Teacher Interviews. Stowell, Mary Anne, Portland Public Schools, OR, 1978, 16p (ED 162 479; Reprint: EDRS).

The last in a series of reports from a project concerning mainstreaming handicapped students in vocational education programs presents results of interviews with orthopedically handicapped, hearing impaired, mildly retarded, emotionally handicapped, and visually impaired students; their parents; and special education teachers and counselors. Survey findings are discussed, and are said to indicate that a high percentage of the handicapped Ss were mainstreamed into the regular school curriculum, that all students expected to be employed at some point, and that both parents and students tended to be uninformed about vocational education offerings in the school district.

59. IEP's: The State of the Art — 1978. Schenck, Susan J.; Levy, William K., Northeast Regional Resource Center, Hightstown, NJ, Apr 1979, 22p. Sponsoring agency: Bureau of Education for the Handicapped (DHEW/OE), Washington, DC (ED 175 201; Reprint: EDRS).

Three hundred individualized education programs (IEPs) and corresponding psychoeducational assessments were collected from the files of children who had been identified as educable mentally retarded (EMR), emotionally disturbed (ED), learning disabled (LD), and other. Frequency distributions were performed on the data obtained from the IEPs and psychoeducational assessments to determine the extent to which required IEP components were actually contained in the programs. Among results were that 64 percent of the cases examined did not report current level(s) of performance; 20 percent did not reveal goals and/or objectives; 18 percent had no statement specific to related educational services; and 68 percent did not include information on the amount of time to be spent in regular education. Other results included that the referring teacher was involved in IEP development only 15 percent of the time; and parents and school psychologists were involved in only 26 percent of the cases. Findings emphasized the need for inservice training regarding necessary IEP components and translating diagnostic information into an appropriate educational program.

60. Implementing Public Law 94-142 in Public Schools in Oregon.* Pyne, Charles William, Brigham Young University, 1978, 163p (7823417; Reprint: DC).

Public Law 94-142 went into effect on October 1, 1977. During the 1977-78 school year a study was conducted to determine which of the law's provisions were most difficult for local school districts in Oregon to implement. In addition to identifying five provisions of the law most difficult to implement, respondents identified three reasons for each of the five provisions selected. Each school district in Oregon was asked to participate. Seventy-eight percent responded. The five provisions of P.L. 94-142 most frequently identified were (1) providing special education personnel; (2) providing diagnostic assessment; (3) developing individual education programs (IEPs); (4) conducting staff development/ inservice programs; and (5) involving parents in the development of their children's IEPs. The reasons most often given were (1) lack of funds; (2) lack of special education personnel; (3) lack of preparation time; (4) lack of training; (5) misunderstanding of the law's provisions.

61. Mainstreaming: A River to Nowhere or a Promising Current? A Special Report to the AFT Task Force on Education Issues. Rauth, Marilyn, American Federation of Teachers, Washington, DC, 1978, 12p; small print may be marginally legible (ED 162 976; Reprint: EDRS; also available from American Federation of Teachers/AFL-CIO, 11 Dupont Circle, NW, Washington, DC 20036).

Potential promises and problems in the placing of children with special needs or handicaps in the regular classroom are examined in this document. The history of mainstreaming, its rationale, and generally accepted definition are outlined. The focus of this report is upon the role of the teacher union in the complex requirements involved in mainstreaming. The positions adopted by the American Federation of Teachers and other educational groups are presented. It is pointed out that the best interests of the children who are placed in regular classrooms despite handicaps are best served when teachers are fully prepared and understand their obligations, responsibilities, and reliable sources of support.

62. The New Federal Education Laws for Handicapped Children—Promise, Programs, Problems. Shaw, Mollie, New York City Office of the Mayor, Oct 1978, 78p (ED 176 452; Reprint: EDRS).

The report examines the problems and promises of the new federal education laws for the handicapped (Section 504 of the Rehabilitation Act of 1973 and P.L. 94-142, the Education for All Handicapped Children Act) as implemented in New York state. An introductory section explains the tenets of the laws, including requirements for program accessibility of Section 504 and individualized education programs of P.L. 94-142. The section on implementation includes a comparison of New York's and Louisiana's state plans, a brief consideration of implications for parochial schools, and a description of compliance reviews by the Bureau of Education for the Handicapped. A section entitled "The Reality Factor" surveys such aspects as attitudinal barriers, teachers' unions responses, and inservice and preservice teacher education. A proposal for an outreach program for parents of secondary school handicapped children is included. Among five appendixes is an outline of evaluation, placement, and due process procedures under P.L. 94-142 and Section 504.

63. Perceptions of Special and Regular Education Personnel in Iowa Regarding Mainstreaming, Alternative Educational Strategies, and Responsibilities.* Brown, Jerome, Iowa State University, 1978, 214p (7907238; Reprint: DC).

The purpose of this study was to survey the perceptions of selected regular and special education personnel in Iowa concerning the status of certain special education programs and services. All Area Education Agency (AEA) administrators (N=15) and AEA directors of special education (N=15) were mailed a copy of the opinionnaire. Superintendents (N=100), principals (N=100), special education teachers (N=100), and regular education teachers (N=100) were selected on a random basis and represented the percentage of that group within each AEA boundary as compared to the state as a whole.

A thirty-six item opinionnaire with a Likert type scale and several items asking for maximum class size for regular and special education programs was used to measure perceptions. A return rate of 80 percent was obtained.

Significant differences among the attitudes of the six groups surveyed toward mainstreaming did exist. AEA directors of special education, special education teachers, and AEA administrators tended to cluster as a group and were more supportive of regular education placement for severely hearing impaired children, severely emotionally disabled children, and severely mentally disabled children as compared to the regular education personnel surveyed.

All groups tended to agree with the concepts of cooperative planning and staffing of handicapped pupils, team teaching, and the use of educational aides in programming for certain handicapped pupils.

All groups appeared to support the concept that there should be a limit to the number of handicapped pupils who are placed into a regular education classroom. The teacher groups took a stronger position on this issue.

Further, all groups surveyed tended to agree with the concept of reducing regular class size when handicapped pupils are mainstreamed. Using the Iowa "weighting" system as the base, the data suggested an approximate reduction of seven pupils if a severely handicapped pupil was to be mainstreamed; a reduction of approximately four pupils if a moderately handicapped pupil was to be mainstreamed; and a reduction of two-to-three pupils if a mildly handicapped pupil was going to be mainstreamed.

64. Preschool Mainstreaming: Current State of the Art.
Blacher-Dixon, Jan, North Carolina University, Chapel Hill, Frank Porter Graham Center, Apr 1979, 25p; Paper presented at the Annual International Convention, The Council for Exceptional Children (57th, Dallas, TX, April 22–27, 1979, Session W-47). Sponsoring agency: Bureau of Education for the Handicapped (DHEW/OE), Washington, DC (ED 171 087; Reprint: EDRS).

Teachers in 22 First Chance Projects and 110 Head Start Projects responded to a survey focusing on defining preschool mainstreaming, characteristics and social interaction of handicapped and nonhandicapped children, teacher attitudes toward mainstreaming, teacher preparation for mainstreaming, and parent involvement. Results showed that there are basically two types of mainstreaming, the traditional integration of handicapped children into preschool classrooms originally for nonhandicapped children, as in Heart Start, and the reverse, as in First Chance. Findings further indicated that there is a high degree of clarity about what constitutes mainstreaming at the preschool level. With regard to social interaction, both groups (handicapped and nonhandicapped) had friends in both groups, and nonhandicapped children rarely ignored their handicapped peers. All respondents strongly agreed that parental involvement is a key to successful mainstreaming and found that they had enough time to meet the needs of the parents.

65. Progress toward a Free Appropriate Public Education: A Report to Congress on the Implementation of Public Law 94-142: The Education for All Handicapped Children Act.
Bureau of Education for the Handicapped (DHEW/OE), Washington, DC, Jan 1979, 216p; some print is small and may not reproduce well in hard copy (ED 175 196; Reprint: EDRS).

The report describes the activities of the Bureau of Education for the Handicapped (BEH), and state and local education agencies during the first year of the implementation of Public Law 94-142 (Education for All Handicapped Children Act). The report includes findings from relevant studies and court cases, data provided by states in their Annual Program Plans, and information gathered by members of the staff of the Division of Assistance to States during their monitoring activities. The information was organized around the following six questions which serve as the chapters: "Are the Intended Beneficiaries Being Served?"; "In What Settings Are Beneficiaries Being Served?"; "What Services Are Being Provided?"; "What Administrative Mechanisms Are in Place?"; "What Are the Consequences of Implementing the Act?"; and "To What Extent Is the Intent of the Act Being Met?" About half the report consists of appendixes including the BEH notes and study review, the evaluation plan for the Education for All Handicapped Children Act, the special studies funding history, and extensive tables of data obtained primarily from child counts and states' Annual Program Plans.

66. Section 504, Rehabilitation Act of 1973: Implementation and Implications in Oregon's Community Colleges.* Peabody, Judith Ellen, Brigham Young University, 1979, 180p (8000084; Reprint: DC).

Implementation and implications of Section 504, Rehabilitation Act of 1973, on Oregon's community college campuses was studied. A questionnaire, designed to evaluate the extent of implementation of Section 504, degree of difficulty in implementing various areas of Section 504, and resistances encountered, was mailed to all 13 community colleges in Oregon. Respondents at each college consisted of: the board chairperson, the college's president, an administrator of handicapped programs, a full-time faculty member who works with handicapped persons, the personnel director, the director of grounds and facilities, and the campus 504 compliance officer. The findings revealed that the majority of respondents reported total implementation of 504 within the given compliance time-line was possible, that most areas of the law were ranked "1—Easy" to implement with only one percent seen as "5—Impossible." Three main areas of resistances encountered to implementation were lack of funding, lack of knowledge, and other campus priorities.

67. A Survey of Professional Opinion on the Legal, Financial, and Program Provisions and Expected Impact of Provisions Contained in Public Law 94-142 on State and Local Programs for the Handicapped.* Nash, Herbert Dallas, University of Georgia, 1978, 168p (7822332; Reprint: DC).

The purpose of the study was to assess the impact of P.L. 94-142 on state and local education agencies as reviewed by respective directors of those state and local programs. The study also sought to explore the level of difficulty in implementing important provisions of the law as viewed by state and local special education directors. Further each respondent was asked whether such provisions were necessary. Another dimension of the study was to identify points in the law or proposed rules and regulations which might present conflict with law or problems in program practice in state or local education agencies as viewed by state and local special education directors.

Forty-four state and 18 metropolitan directors responded to a survey instrument developed by the writer. The data were discussed descriptively and in terms of variance from the total mean between and among groups. The data also were discussed inferentially in terms of level of significance. Each subsection was analyzed within and between groups and between total groups in regions. Also, yes and no answers were reported by count and in percentage between groups. Finally results of ranking of ten selected criteria as to level of difficulty in implementation were reported in means and standard deviation.

The general conclusions drawn from analyses of the data were that there are differences of opinion between state and metropolitan directors of special education and, also, differences between regions of the country and between state and local directors. Additional conclusions were that: (a) state and metropolitan directors' opinions tended to differ when compliance responsibilities were the assumed responsibility of one group or other; (b) local directors felt that hearing procedures were not realistic or practical; (c) there was no clear indication that state and metropolitan directors of special education differed in their assessment of levels of difficulty in implementing the provisions of the law; (d) a majority of persons administratively responsible for implementation of P.L. 94-142 believe that most provisions contained in the law were necessary components; (3) state directors as a group did not want the full authorization level funded which conflicted significantly with opinions of metropolitan directors; (f) metropolitan directors of special education viewed state agencies as regulatory, more than half the state directors in the southeast and southwest regarded their agency as non-regulatory, suggesting conflict in practice and theory; and (g) both state and metropolitan directors agreed that responsibility for program interpretation should rest with states.

Implications for the study suggest: (a) the present teacher training methods need study, both at the preservice and inservice levels; (b) present practices, including the 180-day school year, the six-hour day, and 55-minute class periods, need to be studied, utilizing action research techniques; (c) that a cost benefit study be undertaken on a case-study basis; and (d) a longitudinal study to determine whether the individual education plan might make a difference in learning opportunities, quality of programming and generally improving life role expectations for such children.

68. Teacher Knowledge of and Attitudes toward Public Law 94-142.* Shelton, Jean Ann, Southern Illinois University at Carbondale, 1979, 88p (8004093; Reprint: DC).

Public Law 94-142, the Education for All Handicapped Children Act of 1975, contains a provision that inservice training of personnel must be conducted to acquaint teachers with the mandates of the law. Furthermore, the state of Illinois requires that districts receiving funds from Public Law 94-142 set aside 10 percent of those funds for inservice training of personnel. The major purpose of this study was to determine the impact of these inservice training efforts through an evaluation of knowledge and attitudes toward Public Law 94-142 demonstrated by special education teachers and regular classroom teachers.

A questionnaire was designed to test knowledge of, and attitudes toward Public Law 94-142. The subjects for this study were 285 special education teachers and 167 regular classroom teachers in 27 counties of southern Illinois. Analysis of variance was employed to compare group means for knowledge and attitude scores. In addition, the correlation between knowledge and attitudes was determined.

Results indicated that special education teachers are more knowledgeable about Public Law 94-142 than regular teachers but the attitudes of the two groups toward the law showed no significant differences. There are significant differences in knowledge of Public Law 94-142, based on inservice training. Teachers who have attended university special education courses, workshops on the law, or a combination of both, are more knowledgeable than teachers who have received no inservice education. In addition, significant differences in mean attitude scores were found for teachers who attended different types of inservice training in the last two years. Teachers who had attended university special education courses or a combination of university courses and workshops on Public Law 94-142, showed significantly more positive attitudes toward the law than teachers who had only attended workshops or received no inservice training. Teachers who had attended only workshops on Public Law 94-142, showed no difference in attitudes from teachers who had not received inservice education.

The two factors, type of teacher and type of inservice training attended in the last two years, accounted for only 16 percent of the variance in knowledge scores and 10 percent of the variance in attitude scores. The small variance accounted for by the two factors indicate that there are other factors which are accounting for the variance in teacher's knowledge of, and attitudes toward Public Law 94-142.

Results of the correlation between knowledge and attitudes showed a small positive relationship between the two variables. More positive attitudes toward Public Law 94-142 were held by teachers who were more knowledgeable about the law.

69. Teachers Talk: P.L. 94-142 Reaches the Classroom. A Look at Early Reactions to the Education for All Handicapped Children Act. Pipes, Lana, ERIC Clearinghouse on Teacher Education, Washington, DC; National Education Association, Washington, DC, Feb 1978, 60p. Sponsoring agency: National Institute of Education (DHEW), Washington, DC (ED 150 121; Reprint: EDRS).

This publication documents the firsthand experience of teachers as they work to implement the Education for All Handicapped Children Act (Public Law 94-142). A panel consisting of three regular classroom teachers, two special education teachers, and a school counselor discussed the problems involved in meeting the requirements of the act and possible solutions to these problems. Discussion among panel participants focused largely on the individualized education plan (IEP), the first provision of the act, upon which further implementation rests. The preparation of the IEP, the placement of handicapped children in the least restrictive environment, and the inservice and preservice personnel development needed to write and implement IEPs in both regular and special education are explored. Further discussion followed on the subject of the effects in the classroom, in terms of attitudes and achievement, on both the handicapped and nonhandicapped students.

70. UCPA Affiliates Report Implementation Experiences with P.L. 94-142: The "Education for All Handicapped Children Act." Ross, E. Clarke, United Cerebral Palsy Associations, Inc., Washington, DC, Jun 1978, 18p (ED 165 429; Reprint: EDRS—HC not available; also available from Analysis: Word from Washington; v7, n5, Jun 1978).

Reports from seven United Cerebral Palsy Association affiliates were collected to identify implementation issues and difficulties relating to the Education for All Handicapped Children Act, P.L. 94-142. Data were compiled for the following major areas: the question of related services, the individual education plan, the due process hearing, least restrictive environment and private school placements, coordination with the private sector, public involvement, state responsibilities, funding sufficiency, preschool incentives, and determination of equal treatment. Among findings were that transportation services are frequently inadequate and have harmful effects on the child; failure of the due process system is a major problem in Illinois; and failures to develop inservice training programs for teachers and associated personnel have been documented in Ohio, Maine, Missouri, California, and Maryland.

71. Voices from the Classroom: Teacher Concerns with New Legislation for Serving Handicapped Children. A Report on a Study of Reactions to P.L. 94-142. Engler, Richard E., Jr. et al., Littlejohn (Roy) Associates, Inc., Washington, DC, Nov 1978, 76p. Sponsoring agency: Bureau of Education for the Handicapped (DHEW/OE), Washington, DC (ED 176 437; Reprint: EDRS).

Teacher questions and concerns regarding the implementation of Public Law 94-142, the Education for All Handicapped Children Act, were examined in visits to six local education agencies (LEAs). Types of LEAs visited included an eastern township, a southwest city, a midwest city, a remote town, and an eastern metropolis. Chapters of the report focus on the problems posed by Public Law 94-142, the settings of the visited LEAs, the teachers and their concerns, typologies of concerned teachers, and lessons learned and recommendations. Among conclusions resulting from the visits and contacts with educators are the following: that priorities of teachers are weighted by their sense of professional values and practices, that information about Public Law 94-142 has spread with great unevenness, that LEAs vary greatly in their support of teams of teachers working together on educational problems at the building level, that LEAs vary in the ways they facilitate working relationships between regular and special education teachers, and

that an audit process can possibly hinder and weaken resources for education of the handicapped. The following recommendations to the Bureau of Education for the Handicapped resulted from the study: (1) create a forum for building knowledge and sharing experiences, (2) create a teachers review body at the LEA level, (3) create regional assistance teams, (4) develop and disseminate guidelines on documentation and IEP (individualized education program), and (5) create policy review offices at the national level for developing and disseminating policy positions. An appendix describes the evolution of study methodology.

BOOKS

72. Three States' Experiences with Individualized Education Program (IEP) Requirements Similar to P.L. 94-142.† Marver, James D.; David, Jane L. Menlo Park, CA; SRI International Education Policy Research Center, 1978, 43p.

Summarizes the experiences of three states (California, Massachusetts, and Montana) in implementing the IEP (individualized education program) requirements of Public Law 94-142, the Education for All Handicapped Children Act. Findings are presented from interviews with approximately 200 participants in the IEP process and from observation of planning sessions, IEP meetings, and special education classes. Observations and conclusions are set forth for two main areas: IEP development (including identification and referral, preplacement activities, the placement meeting, and construction of the IEP), and the content of the IEP (present level of performance, goals and objectives, services and extent of participation in regular program, dates of services, and evaluation). Among findings discussed are that districts have devised a wide variety of methods and materials in all phases of IEP development; the majority of parents interviewed attended IEP meetings and were satisfied with their participation in the IEP process; and rural or sparsely populated areas appear to have unique problems in developing IEPs.

IMPLEMENTING MAINSTREAMING: BARRIERS AND NEEDED CHANGE

Attitudes: Acceptance of the Handicapped

JOURNAL ARTICLES

73. **An Analysis of Factors Related to the Attitudes of Regular Classroom Teachers toward Mainstreaming Mildly Handicapped Children.** Mandell, Colleen J.; Strain, Phillip S. *Contemporary Educational Psychology*. v3, n2, p154–62, Apr 1978.

Significant predictors of a positive attitude toward mainstreaming include: team teaching, years of experience (negative correlation), courses in diagnosing learning and behavior problems, previous special education teaching experience, special education courses, size of class, and inservice program experience related to exceptional children.

74. **Attitude Is Keystone to Success.** Hughes, James H. *School Shop*. v37, n8, p76–80, Apr 1978 (EJ 180 969; Reprint: UMI).

After reporting the results of a survey of vocational teacher attitudes toward handicapped individuals, the author discusses the importance and implications of teacher attitude toward mainstreaming the handicapped. Viewing the teacher as a behavior model, the author points out the major factors influencing attitudes, describes methods for changing teacher attitudes, and lists constructive attitudes for teachers to adopt.

75. **Attitudes and Mainstreaming: A Literature Review for School Psychologists.** Horne, Marcia D. *Psychology in the Schools*. v16, n1, p61–67, 1979 (EJ 195 722; Reprint: UMI).

Mainstreaming legislation requires that special-needs students participate in regular classroom activities to the extent possible. Studies indicate that neither parents, peers, nor professionals may be expected to hold positive attitudes toward these students or be competent providers of positive growth experiences. Existing evidence supports the need for comprehensive training.

76. **Avoiding Classroom Tokenism.** Lewis, Eleanore Grater; Fraser, Kathleen M. *Exceptional Parent*. v9, n4, pE7–E9, Aug 1979.

One disabled child in a school often becomes a symbol of all children with special needs. In the process the child may become even more isolated than he or she would be in a special school setting.

While all children need to feel special in some way at each stage of development, none of them needs the kind of "specialness" which highlights a whole range of differences. Classmates may try to outdo one another with favors and assistance, but relationships don't flourish alone on constant benevolence.

77. **Children's Response to Differences: Some Possible Implications for Mainstreaming.** Thurman, S. Kenneth; Lewis, Michael. *Exceptional Children*. v45, n6, p468–70, Mar 1979.

Children's response to a handicapped child's differences may lie in earlier and more basic psychological phenomena than simply labels or separating.

78. **Dilemmas, Opposition, Opportunities.** Sarason, Seymour; Doris, John. *Exceptional Parent*. v7, n4, p21–24, Aug 1977 (EJ 171 675; Reprint: UMI).

The authors review sources of opposition to the concept of mainstreaming handicapped children, cite a lack of knowledge among many educators about the Education for All Handicapped Children Act (Public Law 94-142), and assert that a major deficiency in the legislation is the inadequate consideration for teacher education.

79. **Emotionally Disturbed Children and Regular Classroom Teachers.** Vacc, Nicholas A.; Kirst, Nancy. *Elementary School Journal*. v77, n4, p309–17, Mar 1977.

Analyzes survey results of attitudes of 102 regular classroom teachers in western New York State public schools toward segregation or integration of emotionally disturbed children. Also cites research studies which evaluate special class versus mainstreaming.

80. **Improving the Social Status of Mainstreamed Retarded Children.** Ballard, Maurine et al. *Journal of Educational Psychology*. v69, n5, p605–11, Oct 1977 (EJ 182 449; Reprint: UMI).

Educable mentally retarded children were mainstreamed into regular elementary school classes. Experimental subjects worked on a multimedia project with four to six nonretarded classmates. After eight weeks of treatment, the nonretarded children's acceptance of their experimental peers improved significantly more than that of the control children.

81. Integrated Settings at the Early Childhood Level: The Role of Nonretarded Peers. Snyder, Lee et al. *Exceptional Children*. v43, n5, p262–66, Feb 1977.

Discussed are implications of recent studies investigating procedures for structuring peer imitation and peer reinforcement with retarded preschool children in a mainstream setting.

82. Mainstreaming: A Study of the Variables Affecting Teacher Attitude. Larrivee, Barbara; Cook, Linda. *Journal of Special Education*. v13, n3, p315–24, Fall 1979.

An attitude scale was constructed using the method of summated ratings. The scale was used to investigate the effect of selected institutional variables on the attitude of the regular-classroom teacher toward mainstreaming special-needs children. The scale was administered to a sample of nearly 1,000 public school teachers in the six New England states. Results of the analyses indicated that of the seven variables considered, the regular-classroom teacher's perception of degree of success in dealing with special-needs students had the most significant relationship to teacher attitude.

83. Mainstreaming Can Be Hard on the Handicapped and on the Teacher.† *Pennsylvania School Journal*. v126, n1, p29–30, 42, Oct 1977.

Typical reactions of regular class teachers to mainstreamed handicapped students are seen to include favoritism of special students and anxiety about how the other students will respond. Additional problems cited are difficulty in expressing disapproval for handicapped students' unacceptable behavior, and inappropriate comparisons of special and regular students.

84. Mainstreaming of Young Children: Unanswered Questions. Umansky, Warren; Cryan, John R. *Childhood Education*. v55, n3, p186–91, Jan 1979.

This review of findings and methodologies in mainstreaming research emphasizes the shortcomings of past investigative efforts. It suggests that much more information is needed before definitive statements on the educational effectiveness and practicality of mainstreaming can be offered. Research areas are suggested.

85. Making Mainstreaming Work. Gross, Jerry C. *Curriculum Review*. v17, n4, p254–57, Oct 1978.

In this interview, Dr. Gross expresses concerns of administrators, teachers, parents, and children regarding placement of special children in regular classrooms. He suggests that the individual teacher's attitude is crucial in setting up an environment in which constructive interaction between normal and special children can take place.

86. Many Teachers Wonder . . . Will the Special-Needs Child Ever Really Belong? Johnson, David W.; Johnson, Roger T. *Instructor*. v8, n7, p152–54, Feb 1978 (EJ 174 065; Reprint: UMI).

Discusses the teacher's role in helping foster a feeling of belonging in special-needs children. Suggests ten ways for teachers to structure cooperative learning groups.

87. Preventing the Delusion of Uniqueness: Multimodal Education in Mainstreamed Classrooms. Gerler, Edwin R., Jr. *Elementary School Journal*. v80, n1, p34–40, Sep 1979.

The author asserts that mainstreaming, by confronting children with their dissimilarities, is likely to increase the probability that both handicapped and nonhandicapped children will suffer from the delusion of uniqueness. He suggests several multimodal education activities, with wide ranging opportunities to explore commonalities, to prevent this delusion among children in mainstreamed classrooms.

88. The Principal and Parents of the Handicapped. Beseler, Yvonne M. *National Elementary Principal*. v58, n1, p39–42, Oct 1978 (EJ 196 128; Reprint: UMI).

Emphasizes the importance of the attitude of the principal and all school staff members in improving the attitudes and involvement of parents in planning educational programs for their handicapped children.

89. Regular Teacher Concerns with Mainstreamed Learning Handicapped Children. Guerin, Gilbert R. *Psychology in the Schools*. v16, n4, p543–45, Oct 1979 (EJ 210 657; Reprint: UMI).

This study examined the concerns of regular class elementary teachers who were the primary instructors for 51 educable mentally retarded pupils and 196 educationally handicapped children. Teachers were asked to express the degree of comfort or discomfort they experienced while responsible for the special child in a variety of school related situations. Teachers consistently reported more comfort with activities involving supervision and academics than with activities that involved public display of the child's competence. Five different teacher response patterns were identified, and teachers were found to be somewhat less comfortable with the retarded than with the educationally handicapped child.

90. A Review of Educators' Attitudes toward Handicapped Children and the Concept of Mainstreaming. Alexander, Cara; Strain, Phillip S. *Psychology in the Schools*. v15, n3, p390–96, Jul 1978 (EJ 183 042; Reprint: UMI).

Literature is reviewed related to the attitudes of educators toward handicapped children and the concept of mainstreaming these youngsters into regular class settings. Research is also reviewed that documents the relationship between teachers' attitudes toward individual pupils and the differential instructional treatment of children. Finally, efforts to modify the attitudes and perceptions of educators toward handicapped children and mainstreaming are presented.

91. Social Acceptance and Self-Concept of Handicapped Pupils in Mainstreamed Environments. Semmel, Melvyn I.; Cheney, Christine O. *Education Unlimited*. v1, n2, p65–68, Jun 1979.

This article reviews selected research findings relative to the social acceptance/rejection and self-concept of educable mentally retarded (EMR), learning disabled (LD), or behaviorally disordered (BD) students in the regular classroom.

92. Social and Behavioral Characteristics of Mentally Handicapped Students. Kehle, Thomas J.; Barclay, James R. *Journal of Research and Development in Education.* v12, n4, p46–56, Sum 1979 (EJ 212 061; Reprint: UMI).

This review examines the literature on the social and behavioral characteristics of the educable mentally retarded (EMR), as children and as adults, which might influence their acceptance or rejection by non-EMR peers in a regular classroom. Attempts to modify undesirable behaviors are also reviewed. The conclusions are pessimistic.

93. The Teacher and Mainstreaming: "I'm Ashamed to Admit How Angry I Can Feel." *Exceptional Parent.* v8, n5, ps3–s6, Oct 1978.

Based on a case illustration told from the teacher's perspective, the article discusses some of the problems posed by the entrance of the mainstreamed disabled child into the regular classroom, focusing on teachers and students learning to cope with their own feelings about the handicapped.

94. Treating the Regular Class Child in the Mainstreaming Process: Increasing Social Cognitive Development. Enright, Robert D.; Sutterfield, Sara J. *Psychology in the Schools.* v16, n1, p110–18, 1979 (EJ 195 731; Reprint: UMI).

It is shown that both moral judgment and interpersonal conceptions (two cognitive developmental domains) seem to be related to adequate social adjustment. Recent empirical studies have demonstrated success in raising children's level of reasoning in these areas. Direct applications of these recent findings to the mainstreaming problem are discussed.

95. The University as a Half-Way House. Lifchez, Raymond; Trier, Peter. *New Directions for Higher Education; No. 25 (Assuring Access for the Handicapped).* v7, n1, p23–40, 1979 (EJ 205 013; Reprint: UMI).

A disabled student and an associate professor of architecture illustrate from their own experience at the University of California, Berkeley, the role of the university in helping all its members move into a larger world of relationships where categories like "able-bodied" and "handicapped" need not define these relationships.

96. Views on Special Education vs Mainstreaming. Patryla, Victoria M.; Seevers, Kenneth. *Lutheran Education.* v114, n5, p278–84, May-Jun 1979.

The authors look at the advantages and disadvantages of mainstreaming and at what it takes to make the program work.

97. Willingness of Regular Teachers to Participate in Mainstreaming Handicapped Children. Hirshoren, Alfred; Burton, Thomas. *Journal of Research and Development in Education.* v12, n4, p93–100, Sum 1979 (EJ 212 065; Reprint: UMI).

Sixty-seven Georgia teachers were surveyed on their opinions about the most appropriate educational placement for handicapped children, by type and severity of handicap. Respondents were more willing to accept behaviorally and physically handicapped children into their classrooms than they were to accept the mentally retarded.

REPORTS

98. A Comparison of Cognitively and Affectively Oriented In-Service Training Programs in Changing Teacher Attitudes toward the Handicapped.* Rothschild, Ilene Nancy, Columbia University Teachers College, 1978, 108p (7822086; Reprint: DC).

This study attempted to determine the effectiveness of inservice courses in improving the attitudes of regular teachers toward handicapped children. Two distinct curricula were developed to judge their possible differential effects on the attitudes of classroom teachers.

One curriculum, involving a humanistic or affective approach to special education was developed. The assumption made was that teachers who were more sensitized to the needs of handicapped children would develop a more positive attitude towards them. The curriculum was offered in the form of a 20- hour inservice course, entitled *Mainstreaming the Mildly Handicapped Child.* The course was offered to classroom teachers from the New Rochelle School District in the Spring of 1977.

The second curriculum, involving a cognitive or ability training approach to special education, was developed. The assumption made was that the teachers who gained knowledge about handicapped children and how to teach them would develop a positive attitude. This curriculum was presented in the form of an inservice course to White Plains teachers. The course, with the same title and number of hours, was offered during the Summer of 1977. In addition, a control group was selected from New Rochelle Schools. This group was not involved in either course.

All three groups were pretested and posttested on two attitudinal measures. The attitude scales selected were the Rucker-Gable Educational Programming Scale (RGEPS) and the Attitude Toward Handicapped Children Scale (ATHC). Also, biographical data sheets were distributed to all groups to determine characteristics of the sample group. Finally, course evaluation forms were completed by both groups involved in the courses.

An analysis of covariance was performed on adjusted posttest scores for the three groups. The results indicated significant differences in attitude as measured by the RGEPS. Scheffe Contrasts revealed that the posttest scores of the affective group were significantly higher than the cognitive group after co-varying pretest scores. There were no significant differences as measured by the ATHC.

Although significantly better teacher attitudes were demonstrated for the affective than the cognitive group, conclusions must be drawn cautiously. The relatively small sample size, the failure of the affective group to obtain significantly higher scores than the control group, and the absence of random procedures restricts one's ability to generalize the findings to the other populations.

Nevertheless, the study did demonstrate that certain types of attitudes can indeed be improved in a relatively small amount of time. The continued quest for meaningful curriculum designs for inservice education would be recommended. Certainly, the efficacy of curriculum offerings to classroom teachers that would include both affective and cognitive components should be further investigated.

99. Creating Positive Attitudes and Expectancies of Regular Classroom Teachers toward Mainstreaming Educationally Handicapped Children: A Comparison of Two Inservice Methods.* Singleton, Karin Waterman, University of Southern California, 1977.

The major purpose of the investigation was to compare two inservice programs for their effectiveness in creating positive attitudes toward accepting and expectancies for mainstreamed educationally handicapped children, with a sample of 76 elementary regular classroom teachers in a small California School District. The two inservice programs were (1) direct assistance, in which regular teachers were trained by the resource specialists to instruct mainstreamed educationally handicapped students in their classes, and (2) workshop, in which teachers participated in six ninety-minute workshops, with a variety of topics related to the instruction of mainstreamed educationally handicapped children.

The following conclusions were formulated. (1) The direct assistance program was more effective in creating positive attitudes of regular classroom teachers toward accepting learning disabled educationally handicapped students, but not necessarily toward accepting those who were emotionally disturbed. (2) Expectancies for mainstreamed educationally handicapped emotionally disturbed children were higher for faculties with no special day educationally handicapped classes receiving the direct assistance training program than for those who received no training. (3) The direct assistance training program for the faculty with no special day educationally handicapped classes was more effective in creating positive expectancies for mainstreamed learning disabled students than the workshop training program, no training program, and also the direct assistance training program for a faculty with special day educationally handicapped classes at the school.

The following recommendations were made. (1) In the mainstreaming of educationally handicapped children, direct assistance programs should be developed in schools in which no previous special day classes for exceptional children have operated. (2) Educationally handicapped children who are primarily learning disabled should be the first to be mainstreamed. (3) Workshops alone are not recommended to prepare regular classroom teachers to accept in a positive manner educationally handicapped students into their classes. (4) Direct assistance programs in which teachers experience daily interaction with educationally handicapped students, utilizing the support and training provided by the resource specialists, should be the method of implementing the mainstreaming concept.

100. A Curricular Program Using Group Processes to Facilitate Mainstreaming.* Burstein, Myra, Case Western Reserve University, 1978, 221p (7816451; Reprint: DC).

A curricular program was developed which incorporated principles of planned change. Organization Development and group processes; teacher needs as indicated by questionnaire responses; and this writer's professional experience related to education of the normal and exceptional child. The curricular program provided for the development of a classroom environment which would facilitate the integration of an exceptional child by directing, through a gradual development of children's group process skills, pupils' appreciation of concepts related to the acceptance of individual uniqueness. The program's basic objectives related to developing positive peer interactions, expanding communication and accepting individual differences. The program was intended for use in upper-elementary classrooms and was comprised of units complete with all necessary information and materials to allow for maximum ease of teacher implementation. Each unit contained a statement of the general topic; specific teaching objectives; an introductory, motivational class activity; a major activity; suggested follow-up student activities; questions for students' further exploration and/or informal evaluation; topic-related children's reading list; and hand-out material for the specified activities. Teachers were instructed to select and/or modify any aspects to meet their own specific classroom needs. In order to determine if the curricular program had the capabilities of fulfilling its objectives, it was examined and evaluated by a panel of educational specialists possessing a wide range or expertise related to educational needs of normal and exceptional children. The responses from this panel were uniformly favorable. In addition, portions of the curricular program were implemented within a regular fourth grade classroom and provided additional verification regarding the program's potential for meeting its objectives.

101. The Effects of Least Restrictive Alternatives on Relevant Education Role Groups. Larson, Harry J. et al., Contra Costa County Department of Education, Pleasant Hill, CA, Jul 1978, 141p; some pages may not reproduce clearly. Sponsoring agency: California State Department of Education, Sacramento (ED 162 454; Reprint: EDRS—HC not available).

The study compared two groups of fourth grade special needs children differing in mainstreaming experience — one group was currently receiving more segregated instruction than they had the prior year and the other group was receiving less. Variables investigated included measures of their attitude toward school, social acceptance by regular class children, attributes of their individual educational plans, opinions of their parents and teachers toward mainstreaming, and their regular teacher's perceptions of needs in the area of special education. Among findings were that changes in mainstreaming, type of instructional program, and student sex were, for the most part, unrelated to student perceptions of the quality of school life, that parents viewed segregated education more favorably as a way of educating children than did regular class teachers; and that the exceptional children in the sample, regardless of their change in mainstreaming, type of instructional program, or sex, were chosen less frequently by their regular class peers using a sociometric task than would be expected. Appended materials include 1976-77 integration reports for communicatively and learning handicapped students, a copy of the Quality of School Life Questionnaire, and talley sheets for the Group Learning Survey.

102. The Effects of School Principal's Experience on Attitude toward and Knowledge of Handicapped Students.* Pupke, William Robert, George Peabody College for Teachers, 1977, 77p (7731632; Reprint: DC).

The purpose of this study was to investigate the effects of relative experience in the form of an inservice training session in conjunction with grade level on the attitude and knowledge of public school principals presently concerned with mainstreaming issues. Thirty-six principals from two counties in east Tennessee served as subjects for the study. The subjects were randomly divided into experimental and control groups by primary (1-6) and secondary (7-12) grade levels. The experimental groups received an inservice training session consisting of video tape recordings concerning important aspects of mainstreaming by experts in the field of special education. The Rucker-Gable Educational Programming Scale (RGEPS) was used to evaluate experimental and control group differences.

An analysis of variance was conducted on the mean attitude and knowledge scores. Findings indicated no significant main or interactive effects for either experience or grade level. However, several findings of significance were discovered through post hoc analyses of RGEPS scores as a function of type of handicapping condition and degree of severity of handicapping condition. This was accomplished through statistical comparison of the principal's score characteristics with the RGEPS scale.

103. An Evaluation of an Experimental Early Childhood Curriculum Designed to Create an Accepting Scholastic Environment for the Mildly Physically Handicapped Youngster.* Hawisher, Margaret Frame, University of South Carolina, 1977, 70p (7807903; Reprint: DC).

Public Law 94-142, Education for All Handicapped Children Act of 1975, mandates the inclusion of handicapped children into public school educational programming. As a result of this mandate, many students will be attending classes with handicapped peers previously unknown and unseen. A review of the literature indicates that children as young as four years have established attitudes toward the physically handicapped that are not accepting nor positive. This investigator was concerned with the effects of specifically designed instructional activities directed by the first grade classroom teacher and an exposure to a physically handicapped youngster on the attitudes toward the physically handicapped held by first grade students. Three groups of children participated in the study. Treatment Group #1 was exposed to the physically handicapped youngster and participated in daily activities geared to promote awareness of the facets of daily living and the feelings and needs of physically handicapped youngsters. Treatment Group #2 was exposed to the physically handicapped child; and the third group of children served as a control participating only in the pre-post test assessment of attitudes. All of the 133 children in the study were pre- and posttested with the *Children's Attitude toward Handicapped Youngsters* (CATHY) questionnaire. Behavioral data was obtained on the students in Treatment Groups #1 and #2. There was a significant change at the .05 level in the attitudes of the children exposed to the handicapped youngster as measured by the CATHY. Behavioral data gathered indicated a greater acceptance and friendliness toward the physically handicapped youngster by the treatment group involved in the daily instructional activities and also exposed to a physically handicapped child than by the second treatment group who was exposed to the physically handicapped youngster.

104. Mainstreaming — Making It Happen. Overline, Harry M. Oct 1977, 54p. Sponsoring agency: California State Department of Education, Sacramento (ED 149 514; Reprint: EDRS).

Attitudes and mainstreaming skills of 264 educational personnel (regular classroom teachers, principals, and special education teachers) were surveyed. Results of the Classroom Mainstreaming Inventory and the Survey on Mainstreaming indicated that Ss had positive attitudes toward mainstreaming all ten categories of exceptional children (including emotionally disturbed, orthopedically handicapped, and speech impaired). For four categories (intelligence, vision, hearing, and emotional problems), principals had significantly more positive attitudes than regular or special teachers. Ss with one or more years experience with mainstreaming tended to have more positive attitudes than Ss without experience, and rural Ss had more positive attitudes than suburban and urban Ss. Twenty-five items (including regular teacher preparation, use of a behavioral management approach, and positive teacher attitudes toward exceptional children) were rated as important for successful mainstreaming.

105. Social Effectiveness and Reintegration of Mentally Retarded Pupils.* Halpert, Jonathan Jacob, Yeshiva University, 1978, 194p (7816112; Reprint: DC).

This study examines the question of whether previously labeled Educable Mentally Retarded junior high school students can facilitate their own reintegration by employing newly learned social effectiveness skills on their mainstreamed teachers. The study also examines the effects of information and previous reinforcement histories on teacher behaviors toward mainstreamed EMR students. Four hypotheses tested were as follows: (1) Teacher behavior will be significantly more positive under conditions of systematic positive behavior of students toward their teachers than under conditions when all interactions between teachers and students are based only on the previous reinforcement histories of the teacher-student dyad. (2) Teacher behavior will vary under conditions where teachers have been informed that students are employing positive behaviors. (3) Teacher behavior will be significantly less negative under conditions of systematic positive behavior of students toward their teachers than under conditions where all interactions between teachers and students are based only on the previous reinforcement histories of the teacher-student dyad. (4) Teacher behaviors will be significantly more negative toward EMR students under conditions where EMR students are not employing any systematic intervention on behalf of eliciting positive teacher behaviors toward the given student.

Each of 12 previously labeled EMR students were integrated into two mainstream academic classes and then assigned to either a training, bogus, or control condition. Students in the training condition received training to develop their social effectiveness skills and systematically employed these skills on their regular class teachers. Students in the information condition did not receive any training but their teachers received bogus information that the students were attempting to systematically influence their behavior. Students in the control condition received no training. The positive and negative verbal and nonverbal teacher behaviors toward mainstreamed EMR students and paired regular class peers were observed continuously throughout the study by observers who were "double blind" to the study. The data was analyzed by a type I, II, and VI analysis of variance design. The results of the analyses were consistent, supporting hypotheses one, three, and four and only partially supportive of hypothesis two.

106. A Study of the Attitudes of Elementary Teachers toward Exceptional Children in the Mainstream.* Peters, Raymond Samuel, University of Maryland, 1977, 116p (7800396; Reprint: DC).

The specific purpose of this study was to investigate and compare the attitudes of resource room teachers and regular classroom teachers toward their acceptance and knowledge of exceptional children in the mainstream in 43 elementary schools located in Prince George's County, Maryland.

It was hypothesized that the type of teaching experience with exceptional children, the amount of teaching experience with exceptional children and academic course credit pertaining to exceptional children would lead to the amount of positive attitudes (acceptance) toward their placement in the "mainstream." Results indicated that there was no significant difference in the attitudes of teachers toward their acceptance of exceptional children in the mainstream relative to their type and amount of teaching experience. However, a significant difference in the attitudes of teachers did exist toward the acceptance of exceptional children in the mainstream relative to their amount of academic course credit. Resource room teachers were found to be significantly more knowledgeable about exceptionalities of children than regular classroom teachers. They were also found to be significantly more realistic in their attitudes towards the educational placement of these children.

107. Teacher Acceptance of "Mildly Handicapped" Children after Teacher Effectiveness Training (T.E.T.).* Jamison, Harry Joseph, Jr., University of Pennsylvania, 1978, 100p (7816315; Reprint: DC).

The primary purpose of the study was to assess the impact of the Teacher Effectiveness Training Program (TET) upon regular classroom teachers' acceptance of "mildly handicapped" children in their classrooms. TET is an inservice program which provides skill training in communication, problem solving, and conflict resolution.

Subjects in the study were 38 teachers who volunteered to participate in the program. The Positive Reinforcement Observation Schedule (PROS) was selected as the instrument that measured the impact of TET upon teachers acceptance of "mildly handicapped" children into their classes. For the purpose of this study teachers' acceptance was defined as a significant increase in the use of positive reinforcing behaviors toward mildly handicapped children mainstreamed into their classes.

Regular classroom teachers did not demonstrate a significant increase in the observed rate of positive reinforcing behaviors toward "mildly handicapped" children after TET training. The interactive effect of treatment and pre-post observation on the rate of positive reinforcing behaviors was also not significant.

The teachers also did not demonstrate a significant increase in the utilization of "proximity" reinforcers toward "mildly handicapped" children.

There was no decrease in the disparity between teachers' verbalized views about positive reinforcing behaviors and their observable classroom behavior after TET training.

The results indicated that changing these teacher biases about mainstreamed mildly handicapped children could not be achieved in a short term inservice training program. Suggestions for further investigation of the impact of affective education programs such as TET were also made.

Any future success in mainstreaming special education children into regular classes will probably depend on a well-planned, longitudinal program (one to two years) of inservice education assisting regular classroom teachers to work with "mildly handicapped" children.

Roles and Skills

New Role Definitions and Training Needs

JOURNAL ARTICLES

108. College/Rehab Collaboration for 504 Compliance. Walker, Martha Lentz; Pomeranz, Jacqueline. *Journal of College Student Personnel.* v20, n2, p115–21, Mar 1979 (EJ 197 486; Reprint: UMI).

Existing agency and university personnel can plan and implement the mainstreaming of handicapped students in the postsecondary setting. A model for collaboration of rehabilitation counselors and college counselors is detailed; the model calls for counselors to become involved in the total educational setting, or be "mainstreamed," themselves.

109. The Comprehensive Evaluation for Handicapped Children. Hatch, Eric J. et al. *Elementary School Guidance and Counseling.* v13, n3, p171–87, Feb 1979 (EJ 197 549; Reprint: UMI).

Since the passage of P.L. 94-142, it is especially important for counselors to know evaluation methods. This article presents a description of the usual sequence of a total assessment followed by a brief description of the role of each of the team members. A more technical overview of comprehensive diagnostic or prescriptive methods for the exceptional child is then provided.

110. Counseling the Handicapped in the Secondary School Under PL 94-142. Nelson, Eileen S. *High School Journal.* v63, n3, p109–13, Dec 1979.

The author discusses four counseling areas in which the secondary counselor will be highly involved with handicapped students: academic advising; counseling for postsecondary education; career or vocational guidance; and counseling for athletics, recreation, and clubs. Under each heading both legal concerns about discrimination and interpersonal considerations are discussed.

111. The Counselor's Role in Developing the Individualized Educational Program. Kameen, Marilyn C.; Parker, Linda G. *Elementary School Guidance and Counseling.* v13, n3, p189–96, Feb 1979 (EJ 197 550; Reprint: UMI).

Through the use of a case study, the author examines the role of an elementary school counselor and how he or she might be involved in both the development and implementation of the individualized educational program (IEP) with one disabled child.

112. Defining "Appropriate Education": Put the Ball in the Educator's Court. Behrmann, June et al. *Education and Training of the Mentally Retarded.* v14, n3, p238–39, Oct 1979.

If decisions are forced into the federal courts because of a lack of leadership and responsiveness of the local and state education agencies, then federal judges, not educators, will ultimately decide what "appropriate education" is under P.L. 94-142. States must keep these decisions out of federal courts and put the decisions into the hands of local school districts.

113. Educating Handicapped Children in the Regular Classroom: Needs Assessment in Teacher Preparation. Gear, Gayle H.; Gable, Robert K. *Journal of Research and Development in Education.* v12, n4, p36–45, Sum 1979 (EJ 212 060; Reprint: UMI).

The authors report the development of an instrument, the Essential Teacher Competencies questionnaire, and the results of an assessment of regular classroom teachers' perceived training priorities to equip them to function effectively with mainstreamed handicapped children.

114. Enforcing the Right to an "Appropriate" Education: the Education for All Handicapped Children Act of 1975. *Harvard Law Review.* v92, n5, p1103–27, Mar 1979.

This article suggests pathways for legal interpretations of the Education for all Handicapped Children Act, P.L. 94-142. Part I discusses the forces which led to congressional passage of the law. Part II evaluates the act's procedural system and suggests measures for improving its effectiveness as a means of enforcing the right to an appropriate education. Finally, Part III discusses several substantive areas in which complaints are likely to arise: student evaluation, placement decisions, and the definition of an "appropriate" education. This part attempts to illuminate the major areas of potential conflict and to suggest factors that judges and hearing officers should consider in resolving disagreements between parents and schools.

115. The Faculty Role: New Responsibilities for Program Access. Jastram, Philip S. *New Directions for Higher Education; No. 25 (Assuring Access for the Handicapped).* v7, n1, p11–22, 1979 (EJ 205 012; Reprint: UMI).

College faculty can learn to deal with common questions concerning disabled students, such as how much special assistance to offer them, and what special accommodations must be made to their particular limitations. Program requirements should be reviewed in order to distinguish what is essential.

116. Got Those PL 94-142 Blues. Huckaby, Harriette; Daly, Jerry. *Personnel and Guidance Journal.* v58, n1, p70–72, Sep 1979.

Mainstreaming and P.L. 94-142 make great demands on the school counselor, in terms of time and in terms of new roles and skills. Counselors need improved education and additional staff to meet these responsibilities.

117. The Handicapped Child in the Mainstream—New Roles for the Regular Educator. Mori, Allen A. *Education.* v99, n3, p243–49, Spr 1979 (EJ 203 584; Reprint: UMI).

Appropriate educational experiences for handicapped children in the mainstream of education will only occur if regular educators are willing to accept some new professional roles. The article describes some of these new roles and presents a rationale for relying on the regular educator to provide meaningful experiences for handicapped children in the mainstream.

118. Identifying Competencies for Mainstream Teachers through the Perceptions of State Directors of Special Instruction. Monaco, Theresa; Chiappetta, Eugene L. *Education.* v99, n1, p59–63, Fall 1978 (EJ 192 954; Reprint: UMI).

Competency prioritization from this survey of state special education directors resulted in the following: individualizes instruction; comprehends abilities of exceptional and handicapped children; evaluates and diagnoses students' abilities/progress; provides humanly supportive environment; uses behavioral management strategies; works cooperatively with adults; utilizes psychology of learning; evaluates utility of various instructional strategies; interprets task analysis; evaluates resource appropriateness; promotes mainstreaming.

119. Implementing IEPs; Implications for the Principal. Dougherty, John W. *NASSP Bulletin.* v63, n431, p49–54, Dec 1979 (EJ 211 016; Reprint: UMI).

The author describes the process of implementing the IEP and Least Restrictive Environment and considers the principal's responsibilities in a mainstreaming program.

120. In Physical Education Programs: The Implications of Mainstreaming Handicapped Children. Dummer, Gail M.; Semmel, Melvyn I. *Viewpoints.* v53, n2, p89–102, Mar 1977.

The 1978 deadline for implementation of the Education for All Handicapped Children Act (P.L. 94-142) requires that physical educators act immediately to develop appropriate instructional programs for both mildly and severely handicapped children and to train personnel with the expertise needed to deliver these programs.

121. Individual Competencies Needed to Implement P.L. 94-142. Haisley, Fay B.; Gilberts, Robert D. *Journal of Teacher Education.* v29, n6, p30–33, Nov-Dec 1978 (EJ 193 342; Reprint: UMI).

A checklist of teacher knowledge and skill competencies that should be acquired for successfully teaching handicapped students is presented.

122. Individualized Mainstreaming: Another Option for Principals. Roubinek, Darrell L. *National Elementary Principal.* v56, n6, p43–46, Jul–Aug 1977.

The underlying ingredient of individualized mainstreaming is inclusion, not separation, on a long-term basis. The policy of inclusion encourages grouping patterns that allow children who are different in many ways to live and learn together when it is of benefit to them. The advantages of mainstreaming and the implications of individualized mainstreaming for teacher roles are discussed.

123. The Interface between Regular and Special Education. Reynolds, Maynard C.; Birch, Jack W. *Teacher Education and Special Education.* v1, n1, p12–27, Fall 1977 (available from Teacher Education and Special Education, The Council for Exceptional Children, 1920 Association Drive, Reston, VA 22091).

The authors suggest 12 areas for developing mainstream programs in which regular and special educators can work together.

124. Issues Regarding the IEP: Teachers on the Front Line. Hayes, Josephine; Higgins, Scottie Torres. *Exceptional Children.* v44, n4, p267–73, Jan 1978.

The authors explore how Public Law 94-142 (Education for All Handicapped Children Act) makes teachers responsible and accountable for assuring that each handicapped child receive the required special education and related services set forth in the individualized education program.

125. Mainstreaming: Too Often a Myth, Too Rarely a Reality. McIntosh, Dean K. *Academic Therapy.* v15, n1, p53–59, Sep 1979.

Rarely do educators today serve as true innovators. More often they are reactors to the pressing demands of parents, the community, and lately, the courts. In many cases, mainstreaming has suffered from this emphasis on immediate reaction; too often, special classes have simply been shut down. If mainstreaming is to work, total commitment is required from all, as are public relations efforts and a well-developed reeducation plan for both regular and special class teachers.

126. Mainstreaming Competency Specifications for Elementary Teachers. Redden, Martha Ross; Blackhurst, A. Edward. *Exceptional Children.* v44, n8, p615–17, May 1978.

Surveys of 184 elementary teachers involved in mainstreaming of handicapped children identified 271 specific tasks, 32 competency statements, and 6 broader categories related to mainstreaming.

127. Mainstreaming Exceptional Teachers. Vandivier, Stella Sue; Vandivier, Phillip L. *Clearing House*. v52, n9, p458–59, May 1979 (EJ 202 550; Reprint: UMI).

Special educators cannot afford to alienate regular teachers, for to do so is perhaps to win the battle and gain a few minor . concessions for specific exceptional students, but lose the war in terms of teacher receptivity to mainstreaming. Change should be gently nurtured rather than abruptly forced.

128. Mainstreaming Parents of the Handicapped. Karnes, Merle B. *Teacher*. v95, n2, p90–91, Oct 1977 (EJ 179 927; Reprint: UMI).

Mainstreaming handicapped children is becoming standard educational practice. However, involving parents of handicapped and nonhandicapped children in a mainstreaming program requires special efforts on the part of the teacher. Suggests some guidelines for building attitudes of parents and for learning about other parent-involvement programs and includes seven skills needed for teachers to work effectively with parents.

129. Minority Parent Involvement in the IEP Process: A Systematic Model Approach. Marion, Robert. *Focus on Exceptional Children*. v10, n8, p1–15, Jan 1979.

A tep-step model is presented for improving the participation of minority parents in the planning process for their handicapped children.

130. Obligation of the Disabled Student: Reasonable Self-Help. Pinder, Peggy. *New Directions for Higher Education; No. 25 (Assuring Access for the Handicapped)*. v7, n1, p1–10, 1979 (EJ 205 011; Reprint: UMI).

The responsibilities of colleges and universities toward handicapped students under Section 504 of the Rehabilitation Act of 1973 are matched by the responsibilities of disabled persons themselves toward their institution. Advanced planning by both colleges and students and an end to arrangements that segregate the handicapped are advocated.

131. P.L. 94-142: Responsibility for the Special Education Teacher. Chandler, Harry N.; Utz, Vernon R. *Pointer*. v23, n2, p66–76, Win 1979 (EJ 204 838; Reprint: UMI).

The article discusses the role of the special education teacher in the implementation of Public Law 94-142 (Education for All Handicapped Children Act) and Public Law 93-112 (Section 504 of the Vocational Rehabilitation Act). Forms for the special education teacher to use in observing regular classrooms are included.

132. PL 94-142 and the Elementary School Counselor: An Interview. McIntosh, Dean K. et al. *Elementary School Guidance and Counseling*. v13, n3, p152–63, Feb 1979 (EJ 197 547; Reprint: UMI).

A special educator, a counselor educator, a school psychologist, a resource room teacher, and an elementary school counselor were interviewed to provide different perspectives on such issues as counselor role and training for creating "least restrictive environments" for handicapped children.

133. P.L. 94-142 and the Role of Nurses in Caring for Handicapped Children. Jones, Eloise. *Journal of School Health*. v49, n3, p147–56, Mar 1979 (EJ 208 672; Reprint: UMI).

The school nurse plays a significant role in the education of the handicapped as a result of Public Law 94-142. This national survey reviews state provisions on the involvement of school nurses in the education of handicapped children.

134. The Parent, Teacher, and Child as Conference Partners. McAleer, I. Marlene. *Teaching Exceptional Children*. v10, n4, p103–05, Sum 1978.

Public Law 94-142 requires, in part, that an individualized educational program for each handicapped child be prepared in a joint conference involving, at the very least, a parent, a teacher, and an administrator. This article considers the conference process, roles of participants, and the advisability of including the child.

135. The Principal and Mainstreaming: Ten Suggestions for Success. Cochrane, Pamela V.; Westling, David L. *Educational Leadership*. v34, n7, p506–10, Apr 1977.

If mainstreaming is seen as a team effort, as presented by the principal, the likelihood of success is greatly enhanced. Ten practical suggestions for help are given here.

136. The Principal's Role in Administering Programs for Exceptional Children. Lietz, Jeremy; Kaiser, Jeffrey S. *Education*. v100, n1, p31–40, Fall 1979 (EJ 209 993; Reprint: UMI).

Investigates significant differences between what building principals perceive as their ideal and real influence and responsibility in 27 key operational/decision-making tasks identified by the Council for Exceptional Children. These perceptions can affect administrator-faculty relationships and, therefore, delivery of services to educationally handicapped children.

137. The Principal's Role in Implementing Mainstreaming. Gage, Kent H. *Educational Leadership*. v36, n8, p575–77, May 1979 (EJ 203 064; Reprint: UMI).

There are new requirements and opportunities for educating the handicapped. The ultimate success of mainstreaming depends on the leadership of school principals. Some of the techniques that make mainstreaming work are simply good educational practice, but other skills are also needed: knowledge seeking about this specialized area, teamwork, and attention to interpersonal issues.

138. **Public Law 94-142: An Impetus for Consultation.** Gibbins, Spencer. *School Psychology Digest*. v7, n3, p18–25, Sum 1978.

Psychologists will become more involved in case conferencing, developing individualized educational plans, and case review as a result of P.L. 94-142, Education for All Handicapped Children Act of 1975. They will work on multidisciplinary teams. Four consultation models are described: mental health, organizational process, information giving, and systems interventions.

139. **Public Law 94-142 and School Psychology: Challenges and Opportunities.** Kabler, Michael L. *School Psychology Digest*. v6, n1, p19–30, Win 1977.

This federal legislation has significant potential for change in the profession of school psychology. This review focuses on five major areas: (1) expansion of services to infrequently served populations, (2) protection in evaluation procedures and individualized educational plan, (3) least restrictive educational placement, (4) parental access to their child's records, and (5) parental right to present complaints.

140. **Public Law 94-142 and the Building Principal.** Rebore, Ronald W. *NAASP Bulletin*. v63, n426, p26–30, Apr 1979 (EJ 197 924; Reprint: UMI).

Ways to establish a frame of reference from which a principal may conceptualize and begin to implement Public Law 94-142.

141. **The School Counselor's Role in Mainstreaming the Handicapped.** Cristiani, Therese; Sommers, Peggy. *Viewpoints in Teaching and Learning*. v54, n1, p20–28, Jan 1978 (EJ 182 414; Reprint: UMI).

Interdisciplinary methods through which the school counselor might facilitate the psychological and social integration of handicapped children are presented.

142. **Some Thoughts about Mainstreaming.** Bauch, Marvin. *NASSP Bulletin*. v63, n423, p77–80, Jan 1979 (EJ 192 463; Reprint: UMI).

The philosophy of mainstreaming all students must include the teacher's understanding of the nature of the student's learning problem. The teacher needs specific suggestions concerning alternative methods from which each individual can profit. Administrators can help by identifying and programing students with learning problems and by reevaluating and revising the secondary school so that it focuses on the individual.

143. **Two Teachers and One Child.** Michaelis, Carol. *Early Years*. v10, n5, p56–57, 65, Jan 1980 (Available from Allen Raymond, Inc., P.O. Box 1223, Darien, CT 06820).

It takes both the classroom teacher and the special teacher to mainstream an exceptional child—they have to communicate and cooperate in order to make the program work.

144. **Will Mainstreaming Fit?** Roubinek, Darrell L. *Educational Leadership*. v35, n5, p410–12, Feb 1978 (EJ 173 568; Reprint: UMI).

To date, decisions about implementation of P.L. 94-142, the Education for All Handicapped Act, have not involved classroom teachers. Every decision made without input from classroom teachers systematically decreases the potential of P.L. 94-142 for positive impact.

REPORTS

145. **Considerations in the Integration of Behaviorally Disordered Students into the Regular Classroom: Teacher Concerns and Considerations.** White, Maureen A. Apr 1979, 28p; Paper presented at the Annual International Convention, The Council for Exceptional Children (57th, Dallas, TX, April 22–27, 1979, Session F-68) (ED 171 082; Reprint: EDRS).

The paper presents results of a survey regarding the role of the teacher of emotionally disturbed (ED) children in reintegration of students into the regular classroom. The following concerns which were identified in the study are addressed: (1) objective means of determining readiness for reintegration; (2) clearly defined procedures; (3) clarifications of responsibilities of individuals; (4) guidelines in the selection of the teacher or the classroom; (5) intentional, systematic strategies for facilitating generalization of learning (academic and behavioral) between the ED class and the regular classroom; and (6) inservice training, both for the ED teacher in how to reintegrate students and for the regular class teachers in how to work with ED students. Listed among criteria for determining degree of individualization which can be provided to students are the social environment, degree of structure, and teaming arrangements. The survey of regular and special class teachers is reported to indicate four top priority inservice topics related to ED students—behavioral characteristics, management techniques, teaching techniques, and learning characteristics.

146. **The Handicapped Children Act—P.L. 94-142: Implication for Principals.** Barbacovi, Don R. et al. Jan 1977, 18p; Paper presented at the National Association of Secondary School Principals Annual Convention (New Orleans, LA, January, 1977) (ED 142 000; Reprint: EDRS).

Provided is a frame of reference for considering the potential impact of Public Law 94-142, the Education of All Handicapped Children Act, on school administrators. It is explained that Public Law 94-142 may reshape three traditional aspects of existing school environments: (1) it might be anticipated that the underlying approaches used to accomplish the mission of schools may change; (2) the role relationships between and among educational professionals, social service professionals, parents, and students may change; and (3) changes in the rationale and processes of educational decision making may occur. Due process and procedural safeguards, individualized educational programs, and the concept of least restrictive environment are also considered.

147. Promising Practices in Mainstreaming for the Secondary School Principal. Davis, E. Dale. 1977, 17p (ED 161 189; Reprint: EDRS).

A study to determine the promising practices which a secondary school principal might use to implement the process of mainstreaming was conducted through interviews with 50 principals and a survey of books and articles published since 1970. The principals were asked to state five to ten promising practices they would recommend and their responses were compared to recommended practices set forth in the literature. There was general agreement between the literature and the principal's responses. The ten most often recommended practices included the following suggestions: the principal provides leadership in planning for mainstreaming within his school, the principal informs all the school faculty members of the process of mainstreaming as it is to be implemented in his particular building, and the teachers should be motivated to study and learn the process.

148. The Psychologist's Role in P.L. 94-142: Consultation Strategies with Peer Groups of Handicapped Children. Schroeder, Carolyn S., North Carolina University, Chapel Hill, Aug 1978, 19p; Paper presented at the Annual Convention of the American Psychological Association (Toronto, Ontario, Canada, August, 1978). Sponsoring agency: Public Health Service (DHEW), Arlington, VA (ED 174 902; Reprint: EDRS—HC not available).

The role of the psychologist in the implementation of the six key principles of Public Law 94-142, the Education for All Handicapped Children Act, is one of an advocate and consultant relationship to the school. A strategy for consulting with nonhandicapped peers of handicapped children at the junior high school level was investigated with a semantic differential to assess attitude change. Girls showed more positive attitude changes after consultation and boys' attitudes became more negative.

149. Public Law 94-142: Implications for Higher Education. Gerlach, Kent P. Apr 1979, 19p; Paper presented at the Annual International Convention of the Council for Exceptional Children (57th, Dallas, TX, April 22–27, 1979) (ED 176 435; Reprint: EDRS).

The document describes the Dean's Grant Project at Augustana College (South Dakota) which focused on the implications of P.L. 94-142 (the Education for All Handicapped Children Act) for colleges and universities offering preservice and inservice teacher training programs. Implications of six major aspects of the law for higher education are focused on: the zero reject principle; individual education programs and appropriate education; the least restrictive alternative; testing, classification, and placement; procedural due process and parent participation; and personnel development/inservice training. Also provided is an outline of teacher mainstreaming competencies which include ability to recognize and describe the normal development behavior patterns of children, ability to demonstrate and utilize knowledge regarding classroom assessment procedures, and knowledge of the factors to consider in planning curricula.

150. The Role of the Educational Evaluator in Malpractice Litigation; Stratagems for Change. Kean, Michael H. Apr 1979, 23p; Paper presented at the Annual Meeting of the American Educational Research Association (63rd, San Francisco, CA, April 8–12, 1979) (ED 173 444; Reprint: EDRS).

Recent legislation and court decisions have upheld the right of every child to a quality education. Public Law 94-142, the Education for All Handicapped Children Act, requires that all states provide an appropriate education for all handicapped children. Given that special education is a civil right, it is inevitable that educational malpractice and special education become entwined. Three noteworthy court cases are: (1) Frederick L. v. School District of Philadelphia—involving screening tests for learning disabilities; (2) Daniel Hoffman v. New York City Schools—regarding a four-year-old with a minor speech impediment who was diagnosed as mentally handicapped and never retested; and (3) Doe v. Griles—a class action suit on behalf of 113 exceptional children in the Fort Wayne, Indiana Community School District who were served by only four teachers. To implement P.L. 94-142, schools should provide evaluation services for collecting data on students, deliver full educational services (including regular class placement, appropriate programming, and safeguards), and encourage parental involvement. The special education evaluation unit should provide services related to student evaluation, program improvement, individualized curriculum planning, and recommended research studies.

BOOKS

151. School Social Work and P.L. 94–142, The Education for All Handicapped Children Act. NASW Continuing Education Series #7.† Anderson, Richard J. et al. Washington, DC: National Association of Social Workers, Inc., 1977, 98p.

Presents the proceedings of a 1977 workshop sponsored by the National Association of Social Workers on school social work as it relates to the Education for All Handicapped Children Act (Public Law 94-142). The role of social work in the implementation of P.L. 94-142 is discussed, and the various ways in which school social workers can assist the mainstreamed handicapped child and can prepare teachers and normal students to accept the presence of such children in the regular classroom are reviewed. A complex model of service delivery in which school social workers serve as part of a multidisciplinary team, encourage and facilitate parent involvement in that team, and act as change agents within the system is presented. The role of a social history in special education evaluation is also reviewed. The role of social work skills in mediating parent/school system disputes in Connecticut is described, and New York State's implementation of its own law for handicapped children is discussed, along with related state and federal legislation affecting the lives of exceptional children in the school system. An evolving model of school social work practice relating to P.L. 94-142 is also described.

Rolls and Skills

Training Methods and Materials

JOURNAL ARTICLES

152. **In-Service Preparation for Mainstreaming. A Continuum of Strategies for Instructional Planning (IEP) Teams.** Skindrud, Karl et al. *Teacher Education and Special Education.* v2, n1, p41–52, Fall 1978 (Available from Teacher Education and Special Education, The Council for Exceptional Children, 1920 Association Drive, Reston, VA 22091).

An inservice model for mainstreaming mildly handicapped children is described which combines competitive, accommodative, and problem solving approaches.

153. **Mainstreaming News: Inservice Resources.** Swartz, Stanley L. *Curriculum Review.* v19, n1, p6–8, Feb 1980.

Reviewed are seven texts and/or media packages designed for the inservice training of regular class teachers in P.L. 94-142 and the mainstreaming of handicapped students.

154. **A Promising Approach to Staff Development.** Yarger, Sam J.; Schmieder, Allen A. *Today's Education.* v67, n2, p70–71, Apr–May 1978 (EJ 186 158; Reprint: UMI).

Problems in implementing the Education for All Handicapped Children Act (P.L. 94-142) and the Teacher Center Act (P.L. 94-482) are described. Optimism is expressed over the possibilities of staff development in Teacher Centers to meet the demands of P.L. 94-142.

155. **Training and Managing Paraprofessionals as Tutors and Notetakers for Mainstreamed Deaf Students.** Osguthorpe, Russell T. et al. *American Annals of the Deaf.* v123, n5, p563–71, Aug 1978 (EJ 188 749; Reprint: UMI).

Effective training and management techniques for the implementation of paraprofessional support systems for mainstreamed deaf students are demonstrated at the National Technical Institute for the Deaf (NTID).

156. **Training Professionals and Parents in Developing and Implementing the IEP.** Turnbull, Ann P. et al. *Education and Training of the Mentally Retarded.* v13, n4, p414–23, Dec 1978.

In light of the Education for All Handicapped Children Act (P.L. 94-142), the article explores some training alternatives for both parents and professionals who are involved in the process of developing individualized education programs for handicapped children.

REPORTS

157. **Approaches to Mainstreaming, Units 1 and 2 (Teaching the Special Child in the Regular Classroom). Description of Teacher Inservice Education Materials.** National Education Association, Washington, DC, Project on Utilization of Inservice Education R & D Outcomes, Jun 1979, 8p. Sponsoring agency: National Institute of Education (DHEW), Washington, DC (ED 174 599; Reprint: EDRS).

The described inservice teacher education program is for elementary school teachers who will be dealing with special children in their regular classroom. The scope and sequencing of topics in the program are outlined, and the activities and resources involved are described. Ordering information is provided. A critique of the program is included.

158. **Assist Program 2: Mildly Handicapped/ Mainstreaming. Sourcebook. ASSIST: Associate Instructional Support for Teachers.** Brown, E. C. et al., Indiana State Department of Public Instruction, Indianapolis; Division of Special Education, Indiana University, Bloomington; Developmental Training Center, Aug 1977, 161 p. Sponsoring agency: Bureau of Education for the Handicapped (DHEW/OE), Washington, DC (ED 176 447; Reprint: EDRS; also available from Indiana University, Developmental Training Center, 2523 East Tenth Street, Bloomington, IN 47401; Teachers Guide: ED 176 448, 171p).

The first of two documents designed to train paraprofessionals to work with mildly handicapped students in mainstreamed settings presents information on preservice and inservice education. Four chapters discuss the following preservice topics (sample subtopics in parentheses): the teacher (forming a good working relationship); the students (the labeling process, prejudice, standardized tests, legal rights of the handicapped, mainstreaming); the school (the educational team, confidentiality, school personnel); and the instructional process (program planning). Six units cover the following inservice topics (sample subtopics in parentheses): assessment (formal and informal methods); long-range objectives; short-range objectives (task analysis, chaining); instructional strategies (decreasing inappropriate behaviors, establishing new behaviors, rewarding behavior); lesson planning (common parts of lesson plans, classroom organization); and lesson evaluation (ongoing evaluation, self-evaluation).

159. **A Comprehensive Inservice Training Program to Enable School Districts to Move toward Full Compliance with P.L. 94-142.** Shaw, Stan F. May 1978, 9p; Paper presented at the Annual International Convention, The Council for Exceptional Children (56th, Kansas City, MO, May 2–5, 1978, Session T2) (ED 153 395; Reprint: EDRS).

Outlined is a nine-phase inservice program for school personnel to aid in the implementation of Public Law 94-142, the Education for All Handicapped Children Act. Provided for each phase are a statement of emphasis, objectives, intended participants, and duration and number of meetings. Phases include a 3-hour meeting with Board of Education and community leaders to describe the law (Phase 1), five 3-hour meetings for planning and placement team (PPT) members (Phase 3), six 3-hour sessions for PPT members involved in data collection and development of individualized educational programs (Phase 5), and ten 3-hour sessions on mainstreaming for regular class teachers.

160. **Individual and Group Counseling: A Competency-Based Manual for In-Service Training.** Fagen, Stanley A.; Guedalia, Leonard J., Psychoeducational Resources, Inc., Washington, DC, 1977, 302p. Sponsoring agency: Office of Education (DHEW), Washington, DC (ED 173 688; Reprint: EDRS).

This manual presents the content and activities employed in the inservice course entitled "Individual and Group Counseling," to sensitize teachers and counselors working with mainstreamed students. The manual is designed to develop competency in effective counseling centering around four basic abilities. Module 1 provides an overview of concepts and skills for counseling and helping. Module 2 focuses on understanding and clarifying communications. Skills for responding with respect and empathy are taught in Module 3. Module 4 promotes an ability to use one's own thoughts and feelings, by sending "I Messages" to further trust and acceptance in a helping relationship. The course and modules are intended for regular as well as supplementary teachers, and it is in such a way that the counseling skills learned will be used in the classroom with regular and special students.

161. **The Individualized Education Program: A Team Approach.** Green, Mary, Drake University, Des Moines, IA, Midwest Regional Resource Center, 1978, 204p. Sponsoring agency: Bureau of Education for the Handicapped (DHEW/OE), Washington, DC (ED 169 712; Reprint: EDRS).

Designed as a 2-day staff development workshop on the individualized education program (IEP), the inservice training package presents an activity-based format on a team approach to the IEP. Facilitator notes, information on materials, sample handouts, transparencies, and evaluation forms are presented for seven units: introduction to the workshop; IEPs, P.L. 94-142, and Section 504; handicapped students in the classroom; steps involved in the IEP process; describing present levels of performance; task analysis and behavioral objectives; and completing the IEP. A listing of approximately 50 materials is included on such topics as appraisal, placement, and monitoring.

162. **Individualized Educational Program (A Multimedia Inservice Training Program). Description of Teacher Inservice Education Materials.** National Education Association, Washington, DC, Project on Utilization of Inservice Education R & D Outcomes, Jul 1978, 8p. Sponsoring agency: National Institute of Education (DHEW), Washington, DC (ED 171 688; Reprint: EDRS).

The learning module described focuses specifically on the development of the individualized education plan (IEP) for the handicapped child and is for the use of parents and teachers working together. The scope and sequencing of topics is outlined, and the activities and resources involved in the use of the module are described. A critique of the module and ordering information for resource materials are included.

163. **Mainstreaming the Handicapped in Vocational Education. Developing a General Understanding.** Weisgerber, Robert, American Institutes for Research in the Behavioral Sciences, Palo Alto, CA, 1977, 93p. Sponsoring agency: Bureau of Occupational and Adult Education (DHEW/OE), Washington, DC (ED 142 769; Reprint: EDRS).

This module is intended for inservice training of vocational educators working at the secondary level, and focuses on (1) acquainting vocational educators with the ethical and legal rights of the handicapped to vocational education services; (2) familiarizing vocational educators with particular handicapping conditions, including terminology, variations in severity, and differing capabilities of handicapped students; (3) acquainting vocational educators with the components (planning, instructional design, and evaluation) of vocational education programs for the handicapped and providing illustrations from existing mainstreaming efforts for the various handicapped categories being considered; and (4) acquainting vocational educators with resource and referral agencies and various publications available to aid them in the instruction of handicapped students. A final assessment section provides questions to serve as a check of general understanding of instructional considerations in teaching the handicapped.

164. Mediagraphy on Mainstreaming. Burbank, Lucille. 1977, 15p (ED 144 297; Reprint: EDRS).

Listed and briefly described are resource materials on the mainstreaming of handicapped children, selected for use in the training of professionals, parents, and students. Included are references to 20 instructional materials (filmstrips, slides, and cassettes), 29 films and videotapes, and 30 print resources. Usually provided in the references are title, author or producer, date, and a brief summary of the contents.

165. Mediating into the Mainstream. Haughton, Donna Denney. Jun 1978, 24p; Paper presented at the World Congress on Future Special Education (First, Stirling, Scotland, June 25–July 1, 1978) (ED 157 314; Reprint: EDRS).

The paper describes Project PREM (Preparing Regular Educators for Mainstreaming), a program to develop a training model and materials to prepare regular educational personnel to work with mildly handicapped students, to expand the implementation of the training model, and to disseminate the revised materials within the University of Texas at Austin sphere of influence. Background information is provided on the implementation of legislation which encourages the placement of handicapped students in the most appropriate and least restrictive settings. Major competencies included in Project PREM are listed, and the ten program modules are outlined. The impact of Project PREM is also discussed.

166. A Parent's Guide to the Individualized Education Program (IEP) as Required by P.L. 94-142 (Education for All Handicapped Children Act). Rosen, Roslyn, Gallaudet College, Washington, DC, 1978, 34p; parts may be marginally legible due to small print (ED 166 914; Reprint: EDRS—HC not available; also available from Gallaudet College P.L. 94-142 Program, Gallaudet College, Kendall Green, Washington, DC 20002).

The guide, written in a self-instructional format, analyzes the role of parents in developing an individualized education program (IEP) for handicapped children. The following topics are addressed: an overview of P.L. 94-142, the Education for All Handicapped Children Act; civil rights guaranteed by P.L. 94-142; and development, content, legal requirements, and followup of IEPs. Seven hypothetical situations involving parent participation in IEPs are provided.

167. Preparing for the IEP Meeting: A Workshop for Parents. Council for Exceptional Children, Reston, VA, 1979, 64p. Sponsoring agency: Bureau of Education for the Handicapped (DHEW/OE), Washington, DC (ED 175 183; Reprint: EDRS—HC not available; also available from The Council for Exceptional Children, 1920 Association Drive, Reston, VA 22091).

The 2-hour training package is designed to help parents of handicapped children become productive participants at the individualized education program (IEP) conference. The kit contains checklists and other resource materials for appraising the IEP as it is developed. Directions and reproducible materials for

workshop participants are included in a guide. A sample invitation to families, suggestions for fact sheets and resource lists, and evaluation forms are also given. A filmstrip introducing basic information about IEPs is part of the package.

168. The Principal and Staff Development in the School (with a Special Focus on the Role of the Principal in Mainstreaming). Klopf, Gordon J., Bank Street College of Education, New York, 1979, 97p. Sponsoring agency: Bureau of Education for the Handicapped (DHEW/OE), Washington, DC; Office of Education (DHEW), Washington, DC; Richard King Mellon Foundation, Pittsburgh, PA (ED 168 130; Reprint: EDRS; also available from Bank Street College of Education, 610 West 112th Street, New York, NY 10025).

The objective of this document is to provide the school principal with some understanding of the concepts of adult learning and development and an awareness of some of the processes and techniques involved in a staff development program. Chapters present a paradigm for growth, cover the planning of the staff development program, provide perspectives on understanding adults and their development, characterize ''the enabling person,'' outline approaches to organizing for staff development, discuss ways to present information and explore dimensions of small group interaction processes and their potential for effective staff development. Experiential activities for staff development programs are suggested and formative and summative approaches to program evaluation are explained. New competencies required of the school principal for facilitating organizational change to implement Public Law 94-142, the Education for All Handicapped Children Act (1975), are listed. Although the material can be used by anyone conducting staff development programs and sessions, it is advised that additional material and actual training may be necessary before competency is acquired.

169. Professional Training Activities as a Part of Mainstreaming the Handicapped: An Analytical Survey of the Literature. (Intensive Courses for In-Service Staff Development.) Alvir, Howard P. 1978, 49p (ED 168 254; Reprint: EDRS—HC not available).

The paper is designed to help managers of mainstreamed programs set up intensive staff training courses on mainstreaming. A brief analytic survey of the literature is followed by a discussion of practical applications of mainstreaming (including philosophy, curriculum, support services, and evaluation). The remainder of the paper reviews procedures involved in developing intensive staff development courses. Topics considered include merging several courses into one through the selective use of performance-behavioral objectives, curriculum articulation by objectives, and the transition from teacher-centered to learner-centered programs.

170. Project MITER: Montgomery Inservice Training and Educational Resources (Final Report). Doyle, Phyllis B. et al., Montgomery County Intermediate Unit 23, Blue Bell, PA, Apr 1978, 386p. Sponsoring agency: Bureau of Education for the Handicapped (DHEW/OE), Washington, DC, Division of Personnel Preparation (ED 159 842; Reprint: EDRS).

The final report summarizes objectives and activities of Project MITER (Montgomery Inservice Training and Educational Resources), a program to assist regular educators and administrators who would or might be involved in the education of mainstreamed exceptional children. Among project activities described are development of a workshop training session and establishment of a planning committee to determine inservice needs. Project evaluation findings are reviewed, and shortcomings as well as successes are pointed out. The bulk of the document is composed of 12 appendixes, including sample workshop agenda, evaluation forms for inservice training, a summary of needs assessment data, and a handbook to Montgomery County Intermediate Unit Services for all categories of special students.

171. The Public Law Supporting Mainstreaming (Mainstreaming Training Series). Description of Teacher Inservice Education Materials. National Education Association, Washington, DC, Project on Utilization of Inservice Education R & D Outcomes, Jun 1979, 8p. Sponsoring agency: National Institute of Education (DHEW), Washington, DC (ED 173 347; Reprint: EDRS).

The described instructional materials are for the use of teachers, parents, and administrators who need to be informed on due process procedures and procedural safeguards for implementing the public law supporting mainstreaming. This descriptive report contains information on the contents of the materials and the activities and resources involved in their use. Ordering information and a critique of the materials are included.

172. The Range of Variability: Inservice Design in Special Education. Massey, Sara; Henderson, Robert, New England Teacher Corps Network, NH, 1977, 129p. Sponsoring agency: Office of Education (DHEW), Washington, DC, Teacher Corps (ED 168 234; Reprint: EDRS; also available from New England Teacher Corps Network, P.O. Box 1065, Portsmouth, NH 03801).

The book contains 11 essays presented at a New England Teacher Corps Network institute series on the inservice training of regular classroom teachers and paraprofessionals in the education of handicapped children. Titles and authors include "Ending the Isolation of the Handicapped" (W. Smith), "Perspectives for Staff Development—A Collaborative Design" (P. Mann, R. McClung), "An Inservice Seminar on Mainstreaming—Using Network Support at a Local Level" (V. Trumbull, W. Brown), "The Application of Special Educational Perspectives and Approaches in Regular Secondary Classrooms" (M. Nahmias, A. Allnutt), "The Mini Course—An Alternative Approach to Inservice Education" (R. Glass, et al.), "A Non-Special Education Child Study Team—A Job-Embedded Inservice Training Project" (W. Harris), "Orientation to Exceptional Children through Placement Committee Activities" (P. Sherlock, L. Dolan), "New Skills for Teachers—An Inservice Counseling Skills Model" (W. Mehnert), "Teaching Children with Special Reading Needs" (A. Dyer), "Is Inservice the Answer?" (S. Massey), and "Conclusion—Network Learnings in Staff Development" (R. Henderson).

173. Resources and Training Materials for Implementing Public Law 94-142. Krasner, Steve, Connecticut State Department of Education, Hartford, Bureau of Pupil Personnel and Special Education Services, May 1978, 14p (ED 173 977; Reprint: EDRS).

The representative listing of inservice and classroom instructional materials reflects the increasing attention given to the implementation of the Education for All Handicapped Children Act, P.L. 94-142. Emphasis is placed upon existing commercial and noncommercial products whose objectives focus on the following: development of the individualized education program (IEP), the placement of handicapped children in the least restrictive environment, due process procedures, and effective planning and placement team procedures. Information on each entry includes the title/author/publication data, publisher/price, and a descriptive abstract. Among materials listed are booklets, films, slide/tape packages, bibliographies, and texts.

174. Resources for Schools: 9. Resources for Training Educators of Children with Special Needs. Network of Innovative Schools, Inc., Andover, MA, 1979, 90p; prepared in collaboration with the Massachusetts Dissemination Project. Sponsoring agency: National Institute of Education (DHEW), Washington, DC (ED 176 444; Reprint: EDRS).

The guide provides information on training materials, programs, and organizations for preparing educators to work with handicapped children. Entries include a brief description, cost, and contact address for materials on the following topics: adapted physical education, administration, affective development, early childhood education, individualized education programs, laws and regulations, mainstreaming, parents/parental involvement, regular classroom teachers, resource rooms, severe special needs, speech and language development, testing/program evaluation, and vocational special education. A second section lists training programs and organizations for adapted physical education/physical development, administrator education, arts/environmental design, bilingual special education, early childhood education, mainstreaming, parents and parental involvement, regular classroom teachers, seizure disorders, severe special needs, and vocational special education. Seventeen resource centers and general training sources are listed, and training programs offered by Massachusetts colleges and universities are briefly described.

175. Teaching Children Who Learn Differently. A Course Designed for the Regular Classroom Teacher in Diagnosing and Prescribing for the Learning Disabled Child. Kosko, Ken et al., Oregon College of Education, Monmouth, 1978, 321p. Sponsoring agency: Bureau of Education for the Handicapped (DHEW/OE), Washington, DC (ED 165 388; Reprint: EDRS—HC not available; also available from Oregon College of Education Book Store, 345 North Monmouth Avenue, Monmouth, OR 97361).

Intended as a text to supplement inservice training for regular class teachers, the manual presents information on diagnostic-prescriptive teaching with mainstreamed learning disabled students. Ten sections focus on the following diagnostic aspects: referral, parent involvement, case history collection, assessment of academic abilities and disabilities, observation of learning modalities, auditory perception and language factors in learning, visual perception, psychological assessment, data analysis, and situational analysis. The final five chapters discuss delivering services (including preparing an individualized education program and selecting materials to fit the learning style), and strategies for teaching arithmetic, spelling, and reading.

176. Vocational Education: Teaching the Handicapped in Regular Classes. Weisgerber, Robert, Council for Exceptional Children, Reston, VA, 1978, 89p. Sponsoring agency: Bureau of Occupational and Adult Education (DHEW/OE), Washington, DC (ED 159 852; Reprint: EDRS—HC not available; also available from Council for Exceptional Children, Publication Sales Unit, 1920 Association Drive, Reston, VA 22091).

Divided into seven units, the book provides vocational educational teachers with inservice training on practical knowledge and work skills for working with mainstreamed handicapped students. Unit 1 explores the rights of the handicapped, the capabilities and characteristics of the handicapped, training for competitive employment, shaping the training environment, and evaluating the program. Attitudes that can affect success in teaching mainstreamed handicapped students are discussed in unit 2. Units 3, 4, 5, and 6 deal with individualized instruction for health impaired students, visually handicapped students, mentally retarded students, and students with communications disorders respectively. A plan for action is presented in unit 7, outlining steps for instruction of a specific topic to a specific student.

BOOKS

177. EPIE Report: Number 86m. Teacher Training in Mainstreaming: Integrating Handicapped Children into the Regular Classroom. New York: EPIE Institute, 1978, 107p.

Directed to those who design training programs for this audience—the classroom teacher. Through providing reliable and useful information on the instructional aspects of available materials, we hope to facilitate the effective selection of training materials. This report includes detailed analyses of 15 multicomponent, mediated series of training materials which are relevant to the integration of handicapped children into the regular classroom.

In Part I of the guide, topical areas related to individualizing instruction are listed on one axis of a matrix and the 15 analyzed series are listed on the other axis. Each series is then marked to show which topical areas it covers. The absence of a mark does not mean that a series does not touch upon a topic, but only that — according to the analyst — the series does not provide significant coverage of the topic. Also, the presence of many marks does not imply value, but only content coverage. In Parts II and III, the same procedure is followed for Handicapping Conditions and for Subject-Matter Areas.

178. A Handbook for Parents of Handicapped Children.† Hobbs, Nancy D. Monte Sereno, CA: 1978, 54p.

The handbook details the rights of parents and children according to the Education for All Handicapped Children Act (Public Law 94-142) and the California Master Plan for Special Education of 1977 (AB 1250). Under the heading "Rights and Responsibilities" are discussed such aspects as basic regulations according to P.L. 94-142, individuals with exceptional needs, the community advisory committee, parents' rights, children's rights, due process protection, the school appraisal team, school records, the concept of least restrictive environment, the educational assessment service, and private placement. Referral and due process procedures covered include fair hearing procedures, individual education programs (IEP's), step-by-step procedures for parents, and placement. A separate section is devoted to special help for parents and covers such topics as preparing for the IEP meeting, giving consent to the final IEP, following the child's program, and special pointers and answers to common questions. Lists of references provided include statewide services in California; assessment, prescriptive, and related services; parent organizations; a bibliography; and a glossary of terms.

179. Mainstreaming: What Every Child Needs to Know about Disabilities. The Meeting Street School Curriculum for Grades 1-4.† Bookbinder, Susan R. Boston, MA: The Exceptional Parent Press, 1978, 94p.

The curriculum guide, designed to prepare nonhandicapped elementary school children for mainstreaming, includes background information on the program as well as units on blindness, deafness, physical disability, and mental retardation. Each unit presents a preparation section for the teacher and five components: simulation activities; exposure to aids and appliances; suggestions for guest speakers; lists of books, movies, slides, and videotapes; and class discussion ideas. Also covered in each unit are sample schedules, follow-up activities, and lists of materials to have on hand.

180. Teaching Exceptional Children in All America's Schools: A First Course for Teachers and Principals. Reynolds, Maynard C.; Birch, Jack W. Reston, VA: Council for Exceptional Children, 1977, 782p.

Intended for pre- and inservice training of regular and special education teachers, the textbook offers a mainstream approach to educating handicapped and gifted students. The first two chapters give an historical overview of the development of special education and discuss some of the major conceptual shifts that seem to be inherent in the mainstreaming movement. Chapter 3 focuses on assessment of both programs and students, and chapter 4 considers how student and program assessments can be matched to provide individualized programs for each exceptional student with particular emphasis on the parents' role in the planning process. Seven chapters provide information on the state of the art in the following areas: giftedness and talents, mental retardation, learning disabilities and behavior disorders, physical and health impairments, speech problems, hearing impairments, and visual impairments. Additional chapters cover emerging trends in school personnel roles and instructional procedures; emerging programs relating to early childhood education, child neglect and abuse, drug handicapped learners, and school age parents; and present problems and issues that appear to hold strong portents for the future development of public school operations. For each issue considered, the authors contrast the prevailing practices with preferred approaches. Each of the 14 chapters begins with suggestions for students and instructor on how to develop the topic into a learning unit with additional resources and activities. Appended are the names and addresses of organizations agencies concerned with exceptional persons and information on teacher training materials.

181. A Training and Resource Directory for Teachers Serving Handicapped Students, K-12. Kapisovsky, Peggy M. et al. Washington, DC: Office of Program Review and Assistance, Office for Civil Rights, 1977, 213p.

This directoy is divided into three parts. The first identifies national resources which provide information, literature on handicapping conditions, equipment, and/or inservice education. Part II is a state-by-state listing of inservice training programs for teachers; state agencies; service and consumer organizations; and directories of services. A bibliography of texts and materials for inservice workshops is presented in Part III.

Organizational Change and Program Alternatives

JOURNAL ARTICLES

182. Administering Education for the Severely Handicapped after P.L. 94-142. Orelove, Fred P. *Phi Delta Kappan.* v59, n10, p699–702, Jun 1978 (EJ 181 510; Reprint: UMI).

Administrators trying to implement P.L. 94-142 will face problems in six areas: identification of the students, placement, personnel, individualized educational plans, procedural safeguards, and professional rights and responsibilities.

183. The Administrative Challenge: Compliance by Wit and Reason. Hanson, Gail Short. *New Directions for Higher Education; No. 25 (Assuring Access for the Handicapped).* v7, n1, p53–59, 1979 (EJ 205 015; Reprint: UMI).

Federal regulations regarding access to higher education for the handicapped are considered in the absence of definitive guidance from the government. Topics include: physical accessibility, recruitment activities, admissions tests, financial aids, off-campus housing, and student health insurance.

184. Adrift in the Mainstream? Hanley, Mary Rita. *Exceptional Parent.* v9, n4, pE3–E6, Aug 1979.

The author considers several major problems still impeding the implementation of the Education for All Handicapped Children Act: lack of federal funds; incomplete identification of children needing service; careless placements; lack of support for mainstreamed children; poorly conceived IEPs; lack of inservice training; and hostility from teachers and administrators already in conflict over contracts, evaluations, or resources.

185. Architectural Accessibility: Matching Places to People. Anderson, Richard W., Jr.; Coons, Maggie. *New Directions for Higher Education; No. 25 (Assuring Access for the Handicapped).* v7, n1, p61–68, 1979 (EJ 205 016; Reprint: UMI).

Accessibility requires consideration of the needs of various building occupants, and necessitates matching places to people, instead of requiring people to overcome barriers. Cost effective approaches to making campus facilities accessible, including mobility needs surveys and the utilization of handicapped consumers, are discussed.

186. Campus Services: A Variety of Alternatives. DeGraff, Alfred H. *New Directions for Higher Education; No. 25 (Assuring Access for the Handicapped).* v7, n1, p41–52, 1979 (EJ 205 014; Reprint: UMI).

The director of Boston University's Disabled Student Services shows how institutions can offer equal access to handicapped students through coordinated campus services. Three types of services that a campus office can help assure are: preadmission inquiries and visits, auxiliary aids, and access to recreational activities.

187. Cincinnati Plans for Special Ed. Agron, George A.; Donnelly, James H. *American School and University.* v51, n2, p50–52, 54, Oct 1978.

The model developed in Cincinnati in compliance with P.L. 94-142 demonstrates that a whole system can be made to accommodate the needs of the handicapped at a reasonable cost in facility modification.

188. Components of a Service Program for the Mainstreaming of Hearing-Impaired Students into Regular University Programs. Bevilacqua, Tom; Osterlink, Frank. *American Annals of the Deaf.* v124, n3, p400–02, Jun 1979 (EJ 206 472; Reprint: UMI).

The authors focus on the trends of providing postsecondary education for deaf students on regular college campuses, as mandated by federal regulations and court cases. They discuss the provision of advising, counseling, interpreting, language development, tutoring, and faculty inservice components.

189. The Cost Effectiveness of Two Program Delivery Systems for Exceptional Children. Franklin, Gerald S., Jr.; Sparkman, William E. *Journal of Education Finance*. v3, n3, p305–14, Win 1978.

Compares the cost-effectiveness of two delivery systems for elementary learning-disabled students—the self-contained special learning disabilities classroom, and the regular classroom with resource room or learning center.

190. The Cost of Special Education. *Exceptional Parent*. v9, n5, pR24–R25, Oct 1979.

Summarizes recent cost studies from the National School Boards Association and the Bureau for Education of the Handicapped on the numbers of children being served under P.L. 94-142, the size of the federal financial contribution, costs of residential versus nonresidential placement, and local cost allocations.

191. Cross-Age (Exceptionality) Peer Tutoring Programs: Have You Tried One? Lindsey, Jimmy D.; Watts, Elaine H. *Clearing House*. v52, n8, p366–68, Apr 1979 (EJ 199 160; Reprint: UMI).

Tutoring's academic and emotional benefits for exceptional students are outlined. This is suggested as a method for secondary schools to meet the Least Restrictive Environment (LRE) and Individual Education Plan (IEP) provisions of P.L. 94-142.

192. Design Criteria for Educational Facilities for Special Education Services. Abend, Allen C. *Journal of Research and Development in Education*. v12, n4, p23–35, Sum 1979 (EJ 212 059; Reprint: UMI).

This article describes the development of criteria for the architectural design of school buildings to accommodate the needs of mentally and physically handicapped students. A comprehensive summary of the criteria is included, covering building design and layout, classroom and service areas, furniture, surfaces, and considerations for specific populations.

193. Economic Implications of Public Education of the Handicapped. Henderson, Robert A.; Hage, Ronald E. *Journal of Research and Development in Education*. v12, n4, p71–79, Sum 1979 (EJ 212 063; Reprint: UMI).

The authors estimate the costs to public schools of implementing the P.L. 94-142 and Section 504 mandates. They consider both quantitative costs, due to increased numbers of students with various handicapping conditions, and qualitiative program costs: individualized education program (IEP) conferences, architectural accessibility, due process hearings, and litigation.

194. Evaluating Mainstream Programs: Capitalizing on A VICTORY. Hauser, Carl. *Journal of Special Education*. v13, n2, p107–29, Sum 1979.

Drawing on H.R. Davis' A VICTORY model of factors associated with organizational change, the article argues that accepted models of educational evaluation will be most useful with programs for mainstreaming handicapped children when they are expanded to include critical factors associated with organizational acceptance and successful implementation of innovation.

195. Evaluating Mainstreaming Programs: Models, Caveats, Considerations, and Guidelines. Jones, Reginald L. et al. *Exceptional Children*. v44, n8, p588–601, May 1978.

A variety of practical and theoretical issues pertinent to the evaluation of mainstreaming programs are presented, including (1) a critique of large and small mainstreaming evaluation studies, with emphasis upon the adequacy of models and the insights they yield for improved evaluation designs; (2) problems and issues in the evaluation of educational treatments, including attention to the variables of instructional time, instructional integration, stating goals and objectives, assessing teacher willingness to accommodate the handicapped child, and monitoring child progress; (3) considerations related to appraising dependent measures (attitudes, achievement, acceptance, cost/effectiveness); and (4) a discussion of issues unique to the evaluation requirements of Public Law 94-142. The paper concludes with a presentation of guidelines for developing and appraising mainstream evaluation reports, and the observation that problems related to the evaluation of mainstreaming programs are not insurmountable.

196. An Evaluation of the Teacher Consultant Model as an Approach to Mainstreaming. Miller, Ted L.; Sabatino, David A. *Exceptional Children*. v45, n2, p86–91, Oct 1978.

Two special education resource service models are contrasted for their effects on student achievement and on teacher and pupil behavior. Academic performance gains were equivalent for both models (teacher consultant and resource room), while teacher behaviors were judged slightly better under the teacher consultant model. Both approaches were superior to controls (no service). The parallel academic gains coupled with improved teacher behaviors suggest utility in having both models in operation within a continuum of services. The data support increased instruction in the regular classroom, thereby promoting many of the goals of mainstreaming through education in the least restrictive alternative, improved regular teacher skills, and attenuation of the effects of labeling.

197. From Residential Treatment to Community Based Education: A Model for Reintegration. Goodman, Gay. *Education and Training of the Mentally Retarded*. v14, n2, p95–100, Apr 1979.

A model is presented to facilitate the movement of children from a residential center to community schools. The purpose of the model is explained to break the reintegration process into incremental steps which are expected to make the child's adjustment to a new school situation easier and more successful.

198. Getting Ready for PL 94-142—Model for Support Services to Mainstreamed Hearing-Impaired Children. Nober, Linda W. *Volta Review*. v79, n4, p231–37, May 1977.

This paper details a project designed and implemented by the Clarke School for the Deaf to assist local school districts in educational planning and management of mainstreamed hearing-impaired children. It includes goals and objectives for an outreach program, staff, cost analysis, and assessment of children. The components applicable to P.L. 94-142 and this model may serve to help other schools for the deaf in this regard.

199. The IEP and Nonacademic Services. *American Education.* v13, n9, p23–25, Nov 1977 (EJ 174 914; Reprint: UMI).

Most of the nation's handicapped children do not now receive adequate physical education and recreation services, a situation that can be corrected through individualized education programs.

200. The IEP Dilemma: Obstacles to Implementation. Geiser, Robert L. *Exceptional Parent.* v9, n4, pE14–E16, Aug 1979.

In reviewing potential problems in IEP implementation, the author cites the need to review available support services, to define mainstreaming and the purpose of the IEP, and to exert care that the IEP is a meaningful document with a concrete relationship to the curriculum and the child's needs.

201. An Individualized Learning Disabilities Program in the Regular Classroom. Rothenberg, Julia Johnson et al. *Journal of Learning Disabilities.* v12, n7, p496–99, Aug–Sep 1979.

This article presents a description of and evalutive data on Project MECCA, a nationally-validated model center for the early prevention and remediation of specific learning disabilities. Working with the regular teacher in the kindergarten classroom, the learning disabilities teacher provides inservice training and collaboration in task analysis and instructional goal setting.

202. Instructional Implications of Least-Restrictive Environments for All Children. Roubinek, Darrell; Cheek, Claude W. *Humanist Educator.* v17, n2, p54–63, Dec 1978 (EJ 193 689; Reprint: UMI).

Darrell Roubinek outlines the unique concerns that public and private school teachers and administrators, as well as teacher training institutions, may encounter as they implement P.L. 94-142. Claude Cheek replies that various safeguards and evaluation procedures are the means by which the child's educational opportunities will be protected. Both consider the possibility that the law's provisions (IEPs, parent rights, due process) may be applied to all learners.

203. Issues in Vocational Education of the Handicapped. Weisgerber, Robert A. *New York University Education Quarterly.* v11, n1, p23–28, Fall 1979 (AA 531 008; Reprint: UMI).

This article discusses selected key issues arising from legislation and litigation, instructional practices, teacher competence, and vocational programs that are now, or likely to become, critical to the full integration of handicapped persons in vocational education and subsequently in the work force.

204. Mainstreaming: A Model for Including Elementary Students in the Severely Handicapped Classroom. Almond, Patricia et al. *Teaching Exceptional Children.* v11, n4, p135–39, Sum 1979.

Using the concepts of normalization, mainstreaming, and individualized instruction, a big brother/big sister program was developed in which 16 severely handicapped autistic children (4 to 15 years old) were tutored by nonhandicapped and educable mentally retarded elementary students.

205. Mainstreaming Secondary Students: A Peer Tutoring Model. McCarthy, Richard M.; Stodden, Robert A. *Teaching Exceptional Children.* v11, n4, p162–63, Sum 1979.

A student turoring program in which nonhandicapped secondary students worked with their handicapped peers is described as a successful experiment in reverse mainstreaming.

206. Mainstreaming Students with Exceptional Needs: Implications for the School.† Hunter, Madeline. *UCLA Educator.* v20, n2, p42–48, Spr-Sum 1978.

Mainstreaming, a practice based on the premise that the student with exceptional needs is still more the same than different from peers, is explored. Three possible disadvantages and five advantages of mainstreaming are identified and discussed. Eight school conditions for the successful implementation of mainstreaming (including opportunities for teachers to learn diagnostic techniques, an information dissemination program for parents, and alternate possibilities for placement) are described. Examples of students with exceptional needs who have been taught in regular classrooms are given.

207. Making Time for IEP's. Washick, R. L. *American School and University.* v50, n10, p34, Jun 1978 (EJ 183 234; Reprint: UMI).

Additional teacher time allocations in contract agreements will be necessary to provide the formal individualized education programs for handicapped students required by P.L. 94-142.

208. A Method for Integrating an Autistic Child into a Normal Public-School Classroom. Russo, Dennis C.; Koegel, Robert L. *Journal of Applied Behavior Analysis.* v10, n4, p579–90, Win 1977.

This study investigated the feasibility of using behavioral techniques to integrate an autistic child into a normal public school class with one teacher and 20 to 30 normal children. The results showed: (1) that during treatment by a therapist in the classroom, the child's appropriate verbal and social behaviors increased, and autistic mannerisms decreased; and (2) training teachers in behavioral techniques was apparently sufficient to maintain the child's appropriate school behaviors throughout kindergarten and the first grade.

209. Minimum Competency Testing and the Handicapped: Major Issues. Ewing, Norma J. *High School Journal.* v63, n3, p114–19, Dec 1979.

How handicapped students should be accommodated in the competency testing movement is a major concern that remains unresolved. Specific concerns are: (1) whether minimum competency testing programs should include or exclude handicapped students and if so, to what extent; (2) what criteria or rationale should be used in determining whether handicapped students should be included or excluded from comprehensive competency testing programs; and (3) implications of minimum competency testing for the handicapped. Pertinent legislation from several states is considered.

210. Myths of Mainstreaming. Diamond, Barbara. *Journal of Learning Disabilities*. v12, n4, p246–50, Apr 1979.

The article critiques some of the flaws of mainstreaming, such as grade-level curriculum demands, reporting systems, standardized tests, teacher training, and the individualization of instruction.

211. On the Heels of P.L. 94-142: An IEP for Every Child. Heisner, J. D. *Instructor*. v88, n10, p20–21, May 1979 (EJ 205 312; Reprint: UMI).

An elementary school principal comments on the use of individualized education programs and notes problems to be resolved if IEP's become required for every child.

212. Out of the Regular Classroom but Still in the Mainstream. Larson, Jane. *Instruction*. v87, n10, p99–100, May 1978 (EJ 178 165; Reprint: UMI).

Describes the Knox School for retarded children and discusses the role of special schools in the process of mainstreaming.

213. Playing D-U-M-P or How to Murder Mainstreaming. Wise, James H. *Education Unlimited*. v1, n2, p49–51, Jun 1979.

In a satirical vein, the author describes a game he has created: Designing to Undermine Mainstreaming Programs (DUMP). Any individual or group involved in education is eligible to play and can win specific point scores for the various gambits outlined for sabotaging mainstreaming efforts.

214. Prescriptive Teaching: Delivery Systems for Mainstreaming in Elementary Social Studies. Sanford, Howard G. *Social Education*. v43, n1, p64–67, Jan 1979 (EJ 193 310; Reprint: UMI).

Outlines basic components of a prescriptive teaching program: assessment, curricular objectives, and individualized instruction. Notes the implications that each of these components has for the handicapped student in a mainstreaming environment. Two charts illustrate criteria involved in prescriptive teaching or individualized instruction.

215. Private Schools and PL 94-142. Lehman, William H., Jr. *Lutheran Education*. v114, n2, p70–75, Nov-Dec 1978 (EJ 202 459; Reprint: UMI).

The role of private schools in P.L. 94-142 and mainstreaming of the handicapped effort is outlined.

216. Program Evaluation and the Education for All Handicapped Children Act. Dunst, Carl J. *Exceptional Children*. v46, n1, p24–34, Sep 1979.

Public Law 94-142 states that the impact of programs authorized under the act be adequately evaluated. This article describes the evaluation requirements as delineated in the act and specifies the type of evaluation that is necessary to meet the stated requirements. An experimental evaluation approach is recommended for assessing the efficacy of programs and projects operated under the act. Examples of the use of quasi experimental designs for evaluative purposes are presented.

217. Program Transition for Autistic-Type Children. Handleman, Jan S. *Journal for Special Educators*. v15, n3, p273–79, Spr 1979.

It is the highly structured nature of behavioral technique combined with the demonstrated difficulty with generalization that makes transition of autistic children to more ''normal'' educational environments a necessary, but difficult task. It is important to have cooperation between the current and new placements with a focus on the success of the child. By establishing a network of communication before, during, and after the transition process, chances for such success are increased.

218. S. C. A. P. E. from Stigma: Will Your Middle School Be Ready for P.L. 94-142? Morrill, Leslie Tierney. *Clearing House*. v52, n9, p456–57, May 1979 (EJ 202 549; Reprint: UMI).

Central Middle School in Newark, Delaware, is implementing P.L. 94-142 through its S.C.A.P.E. program, which provides heterogeneous grouping, team teaching, and individualized instruction. The program is coordinated by a resource teacher who plans student placements and works regularly with each classroom teacher.

219. A School-Community Agency Project for Visually Handicapped Children. Vander Kolk, Charles J. *Journal of Visual Impairment and Blindness*. v73, n4, p140–43, Apr 1979 (EJ 204 812; Reprint: UMI).

Describes a model project providing assessment and supportive services for ''mainstreamed'' visually handicapped children. The Albany Association of the Blind contributed professional staff to work in a five-county area for the purpose of educating parents and school staff concerning the needs of children. The goals, team concept, assessment, service, workshops, and evaluation of the project are covered.

220. Science and Special Students. Bennett, Lloyd M. *Science and Children*. v15, n4, p12–14, Jan 1978.

This study was designed to determine if special elementary students could learn basic science concepts. Students included the physically handicapped, emotionally disturbed, educable mentally retarded, and trainables. Modules with pretest and posttest were used. Results indicated that regardless of handicap, students were able to work successfully and adequately in science.

221. **Successful Secondary School Strategies for Exceptional Youth: A Conversation with Ernest A. Gotts and Katherine E. Hargrove.** Hawkins-Shepard, Charlotte. *Education and Training of the Mentally Retarded.* v14, n1, p34–38, Feb 1979.

An interview with university professor E. Gotts and regular education teacher K. Hargrove focuses on mainstreaming mildly handicapped students at the secondary level.

222. **TMH Students Move to Regular Classrooms.** Sutton, Donald. *Pointer.* v23, n2, p50–51, Win 1979.

Briefly describes a Hastings, Nebraska, program in which special classes for the Trainable Mentally Handicapped are housed in regular schools.

223. **Teachers' Preferences for Resource Services.** Gickling, Edward E. et al. *Exceptional Children.* v45, n6, p442–49, Mar 1979.

A study of 121 administrators' and regular and resource teachers' preferences regarding inservice training, cooperative planning, and resource programs for handicapped children was undertaken using an open ended Delphi-type questionnaire and a second, forced choice questionnaire.

224. **Teaching Regular Class Material to Special Education Students.** Breuning, Stephen E.; Regan, John T. *Exceptional Children.* v45, n3, p180–87, Nov 1978.

Instructional academic material was used with 125 students, randomly selected from the first level regular class course offerings of a suburban Chicago high school. There were four phases and a retention test. The results suggest that with the proper teaching procedure and proper incentive motivation, many special education students are capable of acceptable performance on regular class academic material. The procedure used in the incentive conditions did not greatly increase the amount of teacher preparation time; did not require the specialists and aides to become skilled in the principles of behavior analysis; allowed for a substantial amount of individualized and small group instruction; helped to promote the development of social skills; and was inexpensive.

225. **Teaching Secondary Learning Disabled Students in the Mainstream.** Laurie, Theresa E. et al. *Learning Disability Quarterly.* v1, n4, p62–72, Fall 1978.

There is a rational approach to meeting the needs of mainstreamed learning disabled secondary students.

226. **To Sink or Swim in the Mainstream.** Vandivier, Stella Sue; Vandivier, Phillip L. *Clearing House.* v52, n6, p277–79, Feb 1979 (EJ 199 140; Reprint: UMI).

The authors review some of the shortcomings in schools trying to translate mainstreaming theory into practice: lack of a full range of special placement options, over-reliance on consultation and resource teacher programs, and failure to furnish adequate special instruction in regular classrooms.

227. **Usability and Hearing Impairment.** Newby, Jim L. *Teaching Exceptional Children.* v11, n4, p144–45, Sum 1979.

Ambiguities of Section 504 regulations (Rehabilitation Act of 1973) regarding accessibility and usability are cited, and implications are drawn for hearing impaired persons. It is explained that an educational or business facility may be accessible to the hearing impaired but still unusable.

228. **The Use of Volunteers and Parents in Mainstreaming.** Karnes, Merle B. *Viewpoints in Teaching and Learning.* v55, n3, p44–56, Sum 1979 (EJ 208 703; Reprint: UMI).

Feasible ways of mainstreaming the preschool child are viewed, and alternative ways of using volunteers and parents in this effort are delineated.

229. **Use the Handicapped Law to Help Educate Nonhandicapped Kids, Too.** Mills, Pamela Jean. *American School Board Journal.* v166, n5, p29, May 1979 (EJ 201 296; Reprint: UMI).

Suggests applying the provisions of P.L. 94-142 to nonhandicapped students who can benefit from the special therapy and counseling services provided, from the individual education program (IEP) concept, and from the mandated increase in parent involvement. The IEPs and annual program reviews can help boards to reevaluate programs and teachers.

230. **Vocational Education for Special Needs Learners: Past, Present, and Future.** Phelps, L. Allen. *School Psychology Digest.* v7, n1, p18–34, 1978.

This article discusses the state-of-the-art of vocational education programs for individuals with special needs. Barriers which prohibit student participation in vocational education are discussed, as well as legislative developments, exemplary program elements, teacher education, vocational alternatives for the handicapped, and future directions.

231. **Vocational Education for the Handicapped.** Rumble, Richard R. *Clearing House.* v52, n3, p132–35, Nov 1978 (EJ 195 611; Reprint: UMI).

The major characteristics of successful in-school vocational education programs for the handicapped are identified. It is suggested that the most formidable problem in implementing P.L. 94-142 and mainstreaming may be changing teachers' attitudes.

232. **What's So "Special" about Handicapped Preschoolers?** Luetje, Carolyn. *Instructor.* v89, n5, p82–84, Dec 1979.

Describes the program of the Head Start/Developmental Training Center, located on the grounds of the Harbor General Hospital in Torrance, California. It serves 30 preschoolers, half of them handicapped, in a completely integrated program with strong parental involvement.

233. When Mainstreaming Comes In, Are the Poor Left Out? Shiman, David A. *Learning*. v7, n2, p120–21, Oct 1978 (EJ 197 200; Reprint: UMI).

Concern is voiced that in the pressure to spend individual time with handicapped students, teachers will pay less attention to the needs of the nonhandicapped low achievers who come predominately from the poor and the ethnic minorities.

234. Why Mainstreaming Will Succeed while Some Other Special Education Will Fail. Carpenter, William. *Education*. v99, n4, p368–69, Sum 1979 (EJ 206 926; Reprint: UMI).

Delineating problems associated with mainstreaming, this article suggests solutions to the obstacles of: special education classroom environment; parent reluctance; bureaucratic inertia; lack of overall objectives; and failure to use self-motivating techniques with handicapped children.

REPORTS

235. Access to Higher Education: Mainstreaming on the Campus. Ardi, Dana; Palmer, Glenda U. Apr 1979, 21p; Paper presented at the Annual International Convention, The Council for Exceptional Children (57th, Dallas, TX, April 22–27, 1979, Session F-81) (ED 171 031; Reprint: EDRS).

Recent legislation, notably Public Law 94-142 (Education for All Handicapped Children Act), has mandated mainstreaming of the handicapped in educational settings, including the college and university campus. Section 504 of the Rehabilitation Act of 1973 also requires colleges and universities to accept qualified applicants regardless of handicap. The key concept of Section 504 is the principle of access, that is, physical access must be provided by each institution of higher learning. There has been a wide variety of response to this mandate, including such architectural modifications as building ramps, curb cuts, lowering of telephones and water fountains, and wider entrances. Special services and programs are being offered, including brochures and college catalogues describing special programs; personal, vocational, and para-medical counseling; and interpreters for the deaf. Changing misconceptions about the abilities of the handicapped is an important step in mainstreaming this population. Funding for these changes is another major concern of college and university administrators which can be handled by setting up timetables for the needed changes and seeking cost-effective solutions to topographical and architectural barriers. Some handicaps, such as learning disabilities, require academic planning and course modifications. The three major models being used by most universities for delivery of services to the handicapped are: a highly centralized, complete, and direct service program; a highly coordinated, and decentralized program; and a loosely coordinated program.

236. Additional Readings on the Northridge Model of Postsecondary Education for Deaf Students. National Center on Deafness Publication Series No. 3. Murphy, Harry J., California State University, Northridge, 1979, 115p. Sponsoring agency: Bureau of Education for the Handicapped (DHEW/OE), Washington, DC; California State Department of Rehabilitation, Sacramento; Rehabilitation Services Administration (DHEW), Washington, DC (ED 176 481; Reprint: EDRS).

The book describes an integrated model of postsecondary education for deaf students developed at California State University, Northridge. The model uses the facilities and services of a regular university, offering special support services only where absolutely needed to insure the success of deaf students. Lectures are translated into sign language, which has been proven to be as efficient as spoken language. In the 15 years since the mainstreaming program began at Northridge, there has been no evidence of any relationship between degree of hearing loss and academic achievement. Other aspects of the Northridge model covered in the report include a survey of attitudes and perceptions of hearing and hearing-impaired students, consumer evaluation of support services, the educational and family backgrounds of the deaf students, a profile of the deaf students during the Fall semester of 1976, a comparison of the majors of deaf and hearing students, and the relationship between degree of hearing loss and academic achievement. A brief history of the National Center on Deafness is also presented.

237. An Approach to Mainstreaming the Handicapped Child with the Nonhandicapped Child. Orfitelli, Michael A. 1978, 26p; best copy available (ED 164 507; Reprint: EDRS).

The purpose of this investigation was to identify differences among normal children, learning disabled children, educable mentally handicapped children, and trainable mentally handicapped children in motor skill abilities and to develop profiles to demonstrate these differences. Subjects of the study were all educable and trainable mentally handicapped children in the selected public elementary school system, and a random sampling of normal and learning disabled children. Tests in motor skill abilities were administered to each of the groups. Comparisons of these groups were done both statistically and graphically to determine if any differences or similarities existed among them in motor skill abilities that could give direction necessary for mainstreaming them in physical education classes. Findings indicated that certain activities lend themselves more to mainstreaming and others to participation in special programs. It was found that in certain activities normal and learning disabled children should not be integrated with trainable mentally handicapped children. It was indicated that certain groups of normal, learning disabled, and educable mentally handicapped children could be integrated and that other groups of educable mentally handicapped and trainable mentally handicapped children could be integrated.

238. The Assimilation of Two Classes of T.M.H. Children into a Typical Junior High School. Sr okoski, Fred et al. May 1978, 21p; Paper presented at the Annual International Convention, The Council for Exceptional Children (56th, Kansas City, MO, May 2–5, 1978, Session Th16) (ED 153 425; Reprint: EDRS).

Twenty-five trainable mentally handicapped young adults were placed in two junior high schools. The curriculum included communication, basic knowledge, family living and personal hygiene, work preparation, and body usage. Among the concerns expressed by the children's parents were that the junior high youth would not accept the retarded students and that normal young adults would mistreat the handicapped. Among the problems encountered were difficulty ordering suitable materials and equipment, physical facilities in the schools, and policies and procedures regarding such things as field trips, insurance requirements, and general information. After one year, the program was considered extremely successful.

239. The Consulting Teacher Program: Ten Years Later. Perelman, Phyllis F. et al., Vermont University, Burlington, College of Education, Oct 1978, 20p; Light type may not reproduce clearly (ED 164 460; Reprint: EDRS).

A problem designed to train learning specialists called consulting teachers who, in turn, train classroom teachers to educate handicapped children in the regular classroom setting is described. Consulting teacher trainees are selected on the basis of teaching experience, leadership capability, academic promise, and commitment to special education. The process specifications of the training program are composed of lectures, on-the-job practica, and apprentice-like advising. Graduate consulting teachers assist and train classroom teachers to deal with children who are mildly to moderately handicapped.

240. Damming the Mainstream: Barriers to the Implementation of an Innovation. Sivage, Carol, Oregon School Study Council, Eugene, Apr 1979, 19p (ED 175 172; Reprint: EDRS; also available from Oregon School Study Council, 124 College of Education, University of Oregon, Eugene, OR 97403).

The author analyzes mainstreaming (as mandated by P.L. 94-142—the Education for All Handicapped Children Act) from an organizational perspective and maintains that resistance to the demands of mainstreaming is both natural and predictable. Mainstreaming terms are defined, an historical perspective is offered, and hypothetical case studies of handicapped children are given to illustrate representative school programs in three different time periods. Finally, a mainstreaming model is offered which looks at five factors that serve as facilitators and prohibitors of change: relative advantage, compatability, complexity, feasibility, and observability. Ways to overcome barriers to mainstreaming (such as build a reward system) are also considered.

241. A Descriptive Study of Exemplary Mainstreaming Programs: Their Planning, Implementation, and Evaluation Practices and Procedures.* George, B. Vaughn, Saint Louis University, 1978, 131p (7814565; Reprint: DC).

The purpose of this study was to develop the instrument, *Suggested Criteria for the Development of Mainstreaming Programs*. This was accomplished by utilizing data collected from on-site visits to ten midwestern school districts operating exemplary mainstreaming programs as identified by midwestern educational leaders of the mainstreaming movement. Data collected as the result of the on-site visits were combined with proposals, reports, and documents (artifacts) collected. Additionally, information gleaned from the related literature was integrated with the above to compile the suggested criteria. Specifically, the criteria make suggestions regarding the involvement of personnel in the planning and introductory phases of program development, program implementation activities, program evaluation, the role of various school personnel during implementation, necessary inservice education, and the professional competencies and personal characteristics of special education personnel responsible for the delivery of instructional services to handicapped students who remain in the regular classroom.

The suggested criteria were not intended to constitute a checklist school districts must follow to conduct a mainstreaming program. Rather, districts using the suggested criteria should consider it a guide which points to major program and personnel areas requiring specific attention throughout program planning, implementation, and evaluation.

242. The Development and Implementation of a Plan for Mainstreaming Retarded Educable Students into Regular Classrooms in the Comprehensive High School: Phase II. Scott, Walter H., Nova University, Fort Lauderdale, FL, 1977, 216p; parts may not reproduce clearly (ED 168 262; Reprint: EDRS).

The paper reports on the organization and implementation of a plan that assisted 75 mainstreamed educable mentally retarded students meet high school requirements. The report indicates that by the end of the second year 50 percent of all the mainstreamed students received a passing grade in all high school subjects with the exception of physical education. Attitudes of teachers are described as changing positively and parental involvement is shown to have increased significantly. It was established that the students showed significant gains in academic achievement and relationships, and greater participation in extracurricular activities. Among appendixes are sections on helping students develop desirable classroom behavior, various forms (such as a resource room behavior checklist and a due process notice), and a staff development questionnaire.

243. Development and Implementation of an Interagency Program for Emotionally Handicapped Children. Practicum Report. Potter, William H.; Tolley, W. Robert, Nova University, Fort Lauderdale, FL, 1977, 120p (ED 169 689; Reprint: EDRS).

The report, over half of which consists of appendixes, describes the development and implementation of a program in Dorchester County, Maryland, to integrate into a public school 23 emotionally handicapped students (ages 6-13) who had been attending school at a state mental institution. Services provided to the children in the public school program included individualized and small group instruction, behavior modification and contingency management, psychiatric and psychological services, nursing and health services, recreation, occupational and speech therapy, and parental involvement through outreach services. Among the conclusions reached at the end of the program's first year was that the students exhibited a positive attitude towards the program as indicated by improved attendance, the absence of truancy, and the greater degree of involvement in public school activities. The many appendixes include a parental approval form, an inservice schedule, and a list of personnel qualifications.

244. **The Development of an Institutional Self-Evaluation Required under Section 504 of the Rehabilitation Act of 1973, as Amended, for an Institution of Higher Learning.*** Orr, Wayne Shannon, Jr., The University of Mississippi, 1978, 161p (7910474; Reprint: DC).

This study presents information relating to the way one institution of higher learning developed an institutional self-evaluation as required by the regulations of Section 504 of the Rehabilitation Act of 1973 (Public Law 93-112), as amended by the Rehabilitation Act Amendments of 1974 (Public Law 93-516), and presents a model for such a self-evaluation. Procedures and techniques are reported and described as to how an institutional self-evaluation might be made in accordance with the guidelines set forth by the requirements of Section 504. This study should be significant to other institutions of higher learning who desire to develop a self-evaluation of their institution.

During this study, the author served as a member of the University of Mississippi's Committee on Nondiscrimination on Basis of Handicap and worked with the Chairman of the Committee, Dr. John E. Phay, to draft the University of Mississippi's Self-Evaluation as required by Section 504.

In Chapter I is a presentation of the statement of problem, purpose of the study, significance of the study, limitations, definitions, and the methodology of the study. In Chapter II is a review of the related literature through 1977 which pertained to Section 504, the self-evaluation and the transition plan. In Chapter III is described how one institution of higher learning developed an institutional self-evaluation. In Chapter IV there is a presentation of a functional analysis and legal requirements for an institutional self-evaluation of the qualified handicapped. In Chapter V are the summary and recommendations of this study.

Based on this study, the author made the following recommendations:

1. Institutions of higher learning have a well-organized plan for developing the self-evaluation and meeting the requirements of Section 504.

2. Institutions of higher learning that have not completed an institutional self-evaluation should proceed immediately with the self-study as required by the regulations of Section 504 which appear in the *Federal Register* of Wednesday, May 4, 1977.

3. This study may be used as a model for an institutional self-evaluation if information or help is needed in completing the self-study.

245. **Developmental By-Pass Techniques for Teaching the Secondary Learning Disabled Student.** Mosby, Robert J., Franklin County Special Education Cooperative, Union, MO, Oct 1977, 62p. Sponsoring agency: Bureau of Education for the Handicapped (DHEW/OE), Washington, DC (ED 153 380; Reprint: EDRS; also available from Franklin County Special Education Cooperative, Box 440, Union, MO 63084).

Described is an interdisciplinary mainstreaming program for individualizing instruction for secondary learning disabled students, utilizing resource facilities in grades 7-9 in eight separate centers throughout Franklin County, Missouri. Aspects of this program—such as the developmental and by-pass strategies of instruction employed to help students gain the knowledge, concepts, and information necessary to cope with the regular classroom curriculum—are explained. Papers are included on such topics as instructional techniques for meeting the needs of various learning disabled students, developmental by-pass technologies of Missouri Child Service Demonstration Center (CSDC), Missouri CSDC first year research accomplishments, management of a resource room, administrative problems of implementation, teaching literature to the learning disabled student, and serving the behaviorally disturbed/learning disabled student.

246. **An Effective Model for Mainstreaming Emotionally Impaired Students.** Carroll, Julie et al. May 1978, 19p; Paper presented at the Annual International Convention, The Council for Exceptional Children (56th, Kansas City, MO, May 2-5, 1978, Session W3); developed in the Willow Run Community Schools (Ypsilanti, MI) (ED 153 406; Reprint: EDRS).

Described is a ten-step model of services for emotionally impaired elementary students which uses mainstreaming techniques and includes consultation, followup, parental involvement, team coordination, innovative programing, and coordination within the school district and community agencies. The model, which is in full compliance with P.L. 94-142 (Education for All Handicapped Children Act) and Michigan P. A. 198, is noted to focus on the least restrictive environment concept. The teacher's role in the model is outlined; and information on services provided by teachers, procedures and guidelines for placement in self-contained classrooms, the Michigan Special Education Code, and sample forms and checklists are appended.

247. **An Evaluative Case Study of Educational Services for Mildly Handicapped Students in the Mainstream.*** Sattler, Joan Linda, University of Illinois at Urbana-Champaign, 1977, 186p (7804142; Reprint: DC).

The major purpose of this evaluative case study was to describe and analyze the functioning of a ''mainstreamed'' educational program for mildly handicapped students within an elementary school by focusing on particular process variables. These variables involved perceptions and behavioral interactions of teachers and students in three regular classrooms and a special education resource room.

The site of the study was an elementary school of 570 full-time students. The sample comprised three regular classes (including the teachers), a resource room, a total of 18 target students (nine nonhandicapped and nine mainstreamed students), and the remainder of the students in the three classes.

Information was collected over a six-month period within an academic school year and consisted of: (1) background information on the site and sample, (2) behavioral interactions of students and teachers, (3) student peer perceptions, and (4) principal and teacher perceptions of the special education program. These data were collected through the use of ethological observational techniques, administration of a sociometric instrument, interviews with the selected teachers and the principal, and utilizations of documents and questionnaires. Five major research questions were proposed.

Background information of the principal, teachers, and the school milieu revealed that the principal was supportive of special educational services and a positive attitude and team effort existed on the part of the regular class and special education teachers. The naturalistic observations of the teachers confirmed their positive support in working with the mildly handicapped students.

The most revealing finding of this case study was the fact that the selected mainstreamed students were academically and socially adjusted to the regular classes as well as their nonhandicapped, low-achieving student counterparts. The mainstreamed students were *not* far below their classmates in social and academic functioning. However, the selected mainstreamed students and the selected nonhandicapped low-achievers were found to be functioning slightly below the remainder of the students within the classes.

Most of the significant differences found with the naturalistic observations occurred among the three regular classes for the behavioral categories of various verbal student interactions, rather than among individuals. The observations also showed that the structure of the classroom, as to traditional, semi-traditional, and least traditional, was important in grouping children for instruction. The semi-traditional and least traditional classes provided the students with more direct individualized instruction through the use of small groups and more interaction with the teachers than the traditional class. It was also found that the teacher aides were an integral component to the functioning of the individualized basic skill program. The semi-traditional classroom was found to provide the greatest opportunities to the mainstreamed students for improving their academic and social skills.

248. An Integrated Psycho-Educational Program Center. Singh, Surenda P. Aug 1977, 87p (ED 154 599; Reprint: EDRS).

Described is an integrated psycho-educational program center (IPEC) designed to develop an administrative construct for an integrated educational program to provide maximum possible neuropsychoeducational services in the regular classroom for all children identified as exceptional and to provide strategies for developing skills among regular class teachers and special educators within the mainstream of school life. Sections address the following IPEC components: philosophical assumptions; conceptual statement of program objectives; general program description; elements of IPEC; general administrative construct; IPEC activities; general curriculum emphasis areas and procedures; center staff; description of procedures for implementation activities; personnel responsibilities; example of daily schedule; parent-family participation; evaluation; demonstration; advisory council; staff and job description; time-table; and references. Appended are evaluation scales, staff development material used during the 1975-76 year, a staff development identification questionnaire, needs assessment data, an intake form, and a general diagnostic battery.

249. The Least Restrictive Alternative: A Proposed Curriculum Model. Partridge, Don L. Jun 1978, 11p; Paper presented at the World Congress on Future Special Education (First, Stirling, Scotland, June 25–July 1, 1978) (ED 157 352; Reprint: EDRS).

The paper reviews the background of P.L. 94-142 (Education for All Handicapped Children Act) and proposes a curriculum model based on the law's least restrictive alternative concept. Goals of the model are reported to cover three broad areas: student development, organizational efficiency, and accountability. Traditional areas of curriculum planning are seen to include cognitive, psychomotor, career-vocational, personal, and socialization areas. Benefits of the model or profile approach to the least restrictive environmental needs of a child are discussed.

250. Least Restrictive Alternative for Handicapped Students. Information Series No. 143. Tindall, Lloyd W.; Gugerty, John J., Ohio State University, Columbus, National Center for Research in Vocational Education, 1979, 45p. Sponsoring agency: Bureau of Occupational and Adult Education (DHEW/OE), Washington, DC (ED 173 533; Reprint: EDRS).

One of a series of 16 knowledge transformation papers, this paper examines the concept of the least restrictive alternative for handicapped students as it applies to vocational education and provides representative models of service delivery systems. First, the origin of the least restrictive environment concept is traced, including the philosophy behind it, the role of the courts and legislation, and the influences of research and of the search for racial equality. Next, vocational programs and materials are summarized that have attempted to provide least restrictive alternatives for the handicapped. Included are descriptions of the current research literature; textbooks and handbooks; professional development programs; workshops; the role of the paraprofessional; competency-based programs; models for delivery of services; techniques for teaching the trainable mentally retarded; work experience programs; two projects, one in Minnesota and one in Wisconsin; barriers to the successful completion of vocational programs by the handicapped; and the right of the handicapped to employment. Based on the author's experience, three areas are identified as basic to developing least restrictive vocational services: (1) preservice and inservice training; (2) development of a prescription foundation; and (3) teacher preparation for work with handicapped students. Recommendations are offered in the areas of planning, staff development, curriculum, and instructional materials. An extensive list of references is provided at the end.

251. Mainstreaming: The Educational Resource Centers Model. Warrick, Diane Berreth et al., Jackson County Education Service District, Medford, OR, 1978, 345p. Sponsoring agency: Bureau of Elementary and Secondary Education (DHEW/OE), Washington, DC (ED 169 744; Reprint: EDRS—HC not available; also available from Jackson County Education Service District, 101 North Grape Street, Medford, OR 97501).

The looseleaf binder reports on the Educational Resource Centers (ERC) model program in Jackson County, Oregon, which fosters the mainstreaming of mildly handicapped elementary and secondary students (including learning disabled, educable mentally handicapped, emotionally disturbed, and physically handicapped). The ERC provides academic and social skills instruction in order to continue and increase a student's enrollment in regular classes. Instruction may be provided directly to the child or indirectly through consultation with the child's regular teacher. The report is divided into seven sections. A perspective on mainstreaming is provided, including philosophical considerations, a brief review of related research, and an examination of legislation and court decisions. The background and history of the project is reviewed, along with project planning and implementation. Program evaluation is also briefly discussed. The bulk of the report is concerned with program operation, including start-up procedures for ERC teachers, guidelines for processing referrals, individualized instruction, prescriptive programing, behavior management programs, daily monitoring, quarterly reports to parents and teachers, guidelines for termination of educational services, and volunteers. Among the four appendixes are the ERC Reading Skills Inventory and sample prescriptive programs.

252. **Mainstreaming from Plan to Program: From the Perspective of the Mainstream Coordinator. Rationale for Mainstreaming.** Johnson, Florence. Apr 1977, 16p; Paper presented at the Annual International Convention, The Council for Exceptional Children (55th, Atlanta, GA, April 11–15, 1977 (ED 139 228; Reprint: EDRS).

Described is the mainstreaming program at the College Learning Laboratory (at the State University College at Buffalo, New York) to further the temporal, social, and instructional integration of elementary grade mentally handicapped children with normal peers. Discussed are these three components of mainstreaming, requirements for successful mainstreaming (such as a diagnostic prescriptive approach to individualized programing), instructional management, and the importance of providing support services to the handicapped child without his leaving the regular class. Criteria are given for selecting handicapped students for the mainstream program and include ability to work on tasks independently, ability to get along with classmates, and academic achievement adequate for inclusion in some regular instructional groups. Also noted are other program components such as the provision of transitional services to foster acceptance by nonhandicapped peers.

253. **Mainstreaming in the Preschool.** Karnes, Merle B.; Lee, Richard C., ERIC Clearinghouse on Early Childhood Education, Urbana, IL, 1977, 56p. Sponsoring agency: National Institute of Education (DHEW), Washington, DC (ED 152 419; Reprint: EDRS).

This paper presents a discussion of the integration of handicapped children into preschool programs. The paper is divided into five sections. The first section defines some of the terms frequently used in discussions of mainstreaming. These terms include mainstreaming; normalization; P.L. 94-142, the law providing for education for all handicapped children; and IEP, the individualized education plan. The second section presents a discussion of both the legal and legislative arguments used in favor of mainstreaming and the potential benefits of mainstreaming for handicapped and nonhandicapped children. The third section reviews research related to social interactions in integrated

preschool settings. This review includes research on spontaneous interactions, the facilitation of interactions, and recommendations for future research in this area. The fourth section of the paper describes preschool programs which have successfully integrated handicapped and nonhandicapped children. The programs described include center- and research-based programs, transitional programs, and open education approaches. The final section of the paper focuses on the training of personnel, the identification of the components of successful programs, the mainstreaming of severely handicapped children, and arrangement of the environment, and criteria for the evaluation of integrated programs.

254. **Mainstreaming Teenagers with Care.** Kindred, Elizabeth M. Apr 1979, 16p; Paper presented at the Annual International Convention, The Council for Exceptional Children (57th, Dallas, TX, April 22–27, 1979, Session W-25) (ED 171 042; Reprint: EDRS).

The paper reports on a program for mainstreaming acoustically handicapped high school students. Among aspects discussed are criteria for success in mainstreamed programs, itinerant speech therapy services, individualized education programs, and support staff (counselors) roles and functions. The scope of orientation sessions for regular class teachers is described. Seven characteristics of successfully mainstreamed students are listed (e.g., self motivation, good study habits, and high-average or high scholastic ability). Among advantages ascribed to mainstreaming are elimination of bias and misconceptions about hearing impairment and increased socialization. The author praises the parents' interest, involvement, and helpfulness in cooperating with the school program.

255. **Mainstreaming the Handicapped in Vocational Education. Literature Review. (A Research Project in Vocational Education in the Portland Public Schools.)** Rumble, Richard D., Portland Public Schools, OR, Jan 1978, 47p (ED 162 475; Reprint: EDRS).

The first of five reports from a project on mainstreaming the handicapped in vocational education presents a literature review drawn from an ERIC (Educational Resources Information Center) search and responses by 16 secondary school curriculum leaders. The review touches upon the following topics: history, P.L. 94-142 (the Education for All Handicapped Children Act), mainstreaming, the population, specialization, current program models, cooperative work experience and placement, regional support, and aspects of successful programs (such as individualized instruction, flexible grading, and coordinated leadership).

256. **Northville Public Schools/Institution Special Education Program: Comprehensive Administrative Planning.** Rezmierski, Leonard R. Jun 1978, 10p; Paper presented at the World Congress on Future Special Education (First, Stirling, Scotland, June 25–July 1, 1978) (ED 158 512; Reprint: EDRS).

The paper describes the Northville (Michigan) Public Schools' program for providing education to approximately 750 handicapped students living in two major residential institutions. Legislation underlying the program's development is reviewed, operation of the educational program is discussed, and statistics on program staff and students are presented. It is explained that within the public schools, four special classes have been located and mainstreamed into an existing elementary and junior high building, with four individual students having been placed within the K-12 system due to their ability levels.

257. Observations of a Primary School Principal after Four Years of Experience with Mainstreaming.
Sowers, Ganelda H. Mar 1978, 11p; Paper presented at the Annual Meeting of the American Educational Research Association (Toronto, Ontario, March 27–31, 1978) (ED 153 342; Reprint: EDRS).

Mainstreaming the handicapped child requires much more than mere placement in a regular classroom. Careful thought and preparation must be devoted to the affective, as well as cognitive, aspects of classroom experience. This paper describes the mainstreaming program at the North Rowan Primary School in Rowan County, North Carolina. Through team teaching, use of a special resource team, formation of "family" groups of handicapped and "normal" students, and extensive inservice training, the staff has acquired many skills and techniques to strengthen the teaching of basic skills, to assist children in assuming responsibility, and to develop realistic attitudes toward self and others. Mainstreaming and the program devised to implement it have been of benefit to all pupils.

258. A Planning, Allocation, and Distribution Process Under Public Law 94-142.* Howard, Thomas Francis, The University of Michigan, 1977, 127p (7717932; Reprint: DC).

The purpose of this study is to produce a set of administrative procedures to guide the application, allocation, and evaluation of federal funds granted to the Michigan Department of Education for use by intermediate and local education units throughout the state.
The document was developed by breaking down Public Law 94-142 into thirty components. Each component was addressed with relation to clarity and comprehensiveness. The completed document covers all the basic steps for receiving federal funds under Public Law 94-142, from application through drafting the final year-end report. Whenever the recipients of grants have questions, they can refer to the document for an authoritative response consistent with the Michigan Department of Education's policy.
The potential users directly affected by Public Law 94-142 were involved in criticizing the proposed plan. A sample of 28 users who are members of the State Management Task Force were invited to react to the plan. Previous survey research determined that this group of potential users reflected the interests and concerns of the 530 directors and supervisors of special education throughout the state. Seventy-five percent of the comments were incorporated into the final planning, allocation, and distribution system.
Involving management personnel from local and intermediate education agencies in the development of a statewide administrative procedure is a major departure from past state department-field interaction. This is the first time an administrative procedure was submitted to its potential users for reaction during the developmental phase of planning. It is assumed that their involvement will potentially increase the level of acceptance.

259. A Process for Prioritizing Architectural Barriers to Physically Disabled Persons.* Myers, William Leroy, The University of Wisconsin-Madison, 1977, 167p (7728267; Reprint: DC).

The purpose of this exploratory study was to establish priorities of removing architectural barriers in public buildings and their surroundings.
The technique utilized for collecting the data was a structured interview between the researcher and each of eight selected jury members. The jury was composed of the following: two architects, three physically disabled individuals, two of whom were college students, and three individuals with responsibility for providing program needs for the physically disabled. During the interview the jury members were asked to conduct a Q-sort arrangement of their rankings of the importance of removal of the ten major categories of architectural barriers as well as a ranking of each sub-category within the ten major categories. In addition, each member was requested to rank the ten most important and the ten least important sub-categories that would serve the most people. To display the responses of the various jury members, tables were utilized as well as a narrative explanation of the tables.
Selected findings as a result of this study revealed a priority for removal of architectural barriers. The priority list, which is a result of the average ranking of the jury members' responses is presented in order of importance: (1) Access to Main Entrance (2) Doors to Main Entrance (3) Elevators (4) Toilet Facilities (5) Corridors 60 Inches Wide (6) Passenger Arrival (7) Walks (8) Drinking Fountains (9) Stairs (10) Telephones.
Additional findings as a result of this study include: (1) The priorities for removing architectural barriers resulted in four groupings of importance. (2) Access to Main Entrance appeared to be the most important architectural barrier to be removed. (3) Making doors to buildings, as well as the doors within a building, with 32 inches clear opening appear to be high importance to all jury members. (4) The ranking of elevators as an important architectural barrier differed significantly. (5) Doors to toilet facilities and requiring the handicapped toilet stall to be of minimum size was considered very important. (6) Automatic doors were found to have a high importance at the accessible entrance. (7) If automatic doors were not available, then doors with a minimum of eight pounds pressure be required to operate the door.

260. Project Harmony—Success for the Learning Disabled in the Mainstream. Kirsch, Greg, Ingham Intermediate School District, Mason, MI, Nov 1978, 8p (ED 163 721; Reprint: EDRS).

An instructional and mainstreaming model for programming severely learning disabled (LD) elementary students is described, in which students receive instruction for one half of the school day in an LD classroom and are successfully mainstreamed in general education for the remaining part of the day is described. It is explained that components of the model include entry procedure, continuous reassessment and replanning procedures, and time lines; academic and behavioral assessment instruments; step-by-step interpretation of diagnostic data and development of an individualized educational plan; elementary curriculum in reading, mathematics, and written language; well-developed mainstreaming procedures and activities; and materials and forms.

261. Public Law 94-142 and the Minority Retarded Child: An Overview of Issues and Practices. Kendall, William S. 1978, 17p; Paper presented at the Annual Meeting of the American Association of Mental Deficiency (South Central Region, Hot Springs, AR) (ED 169 737; Reprint: EDRS).

The paper examines issues involving the implementation of P.L. 94-142, the Education for All Handicapped Children Act, with minority group students. A critique of studies on minority concerns is presented, and such assessment issues as technical problems and the implications of ability grouping for minorities, are explored. Considerations in evaluating mainstream programs for minority students are analyzed, and suggestions are made to involve minority group teachers, administrators, and scholars in the conceptualization of evaluation efforts, and to pay special attention to the percentages of minority group children in segregated classes.

262. Pupil Selection and Program Development Problems in Mainstreaming the Handicapped Child. Munson, Harold L. et al., Rochester University, NY, Mar 1978, 17p; Paper presented at the Annual Meeting of the American Educational Research Association (Toronto, Ontario, Canada, March, 1978). Sponsoring agency: Bureau of Education for the Handicapped (DHEW/OE), Washington, DC (ED 154 552; Reprint: EDRS; also available from Harold L. Munson, College of Education, University of Rochester, Rochester, NY 14627).

A cooperative approach to mainstreaming between a school for the deaf and a nearby regional Occupational Education Center of the Board of Cooperative Educational Services (BOCES) in New York State was investigated in four programs representing local variations of this model for partial mainstreaming. Three distinct periods of the mainstreaming effort were isolated for study: the period of selection, the period of orientation, and the period of articulation (when communications concerning learner needs and progress are being coordinated between the two facilities and home). Interviews were conducted with 120 administrator-supervisors, pupil personnel workers, and teachers. Among findings were that the need for information about the types and content of courses at the BOCES Centers receives the most attention; that the personnel in both participating institutions make little or no distinction between selection and orientation activities; and that communication between the two institutions does not appear to be a major concern in the day-to-day operation of the cooperative program.

263. A Secondary Resource Room Program. A Practical and Applied Model for Effective Mainstreaming. Wullschleger, Philip; Gavin, Robert T. Apr 1979, 36p; Paper presented at the Annual International Convention, The Council for Exceptional Children (57th, Dallas, TX, April 22–27, 1979, Session W-17) (ED 171 092; Reprint: EDRS).

The paper describes a three level resource room designed to provide a comprehensive program to meet the widely varying needs of handicapped students at the secondary level. An introduction provides the historical background of services to the handicapped. A description of the program includes the organization; the resource room services, such as instruction, prevocational development, and counseling; and approaches to mainstreaming. Operational procedures are stated including freshman intake, scheduling, monitoring progress in mainstreamed courses, reporting progress, parent contracts, administration and planning, record keeping, relationship with guidance, and career education (the CIPED Community Involvement Personal Education Development Program). Appended are descriptions of teacher qualifications, sample schedules, a sample bimonthly progress report, a sample report card, guidelines for resource teacher/counselor responsibilities, sample end of the year progress report, a listing of resource room courses, and sample individualized educational plan annual review and instructional guide.

264. A Special Education Mainstreaming Process.* Babcock, Emery Vernon, Saint Louis University, 1977, 225p (7800470; Reprint: DC).

This study, designed as an experimental program in the state of California, expresses a two-fold purpose: (1) To develop a process for mainstreaming. (2) To implement the process within the framework of the California Master Plan for Special Education and evaluate its effectiveness with respect to three variables: (a) teacher attitudes, (b) parent attitudes, and (c) achievement of children in reading and mathematics.

The mainstreaming process is composed of two components. The five-step budget development process enables personnel to: (1) Assess present special education offerings and transpose them into a mainstreaming program. (2) Project the total amount of state and local funds available. (3) Calculate salary costs for personnel. (4) Develop a mainstreaming budget. (5) Analyze budgetary encumberances and expenditures. The program process includes a ten-step pattern which enables personnel to: (1) Initiate a mainstreaming program. (2) Monitor the program effectively. Each process form is preceded by an explanatory guide. The areas include: identification, referral, case carrier assignment, assessment procedure, assessment analysis, instructional planning, placement recommendations, scheduling, development of learning steps, attendance reporting, and evaluation and recommendation.

The experiment revolves around 14 elementary schools in Northern California. Staff and parent attitudes toward mainstreaming were investigated. In addition, 31 mainstreamed children were included in an experimental group, while 40 served as a control. These exceptional children were given pre- and posttests using the Comprehensive Test of Basic Skills. Finally, a staff questionaire consisting of 11 questions was reacted to by a randomly selected staff.

Findings indicated that teachers, parents, and administrators expressed approval of the program. The children did as well in reading and mathematics as previously. The program recommendations were to: (1) Fully implement the program statewide. (2) Continue to update the process. (3) Require a minimum of two college special education courses for all administrators and teachers. (4) Offer numerous state and local workshops. (5) Develop a research center for special education.

265. Speech and Language Services and the Classroom Teacher. Freeman, Gerald G., Minnesota University, Minneapolis, National Support Systems Project, 1977, 104p. Sponsoring agency: Bureau of Education for the Handicapped (DHEW/OE), Washington, DC (ED 152 040; Reprint: EDRS; also available from Council for Exceptional Children Publication Sales, 1920 Association Drive, Reston, VA 22091).

The author demonstrates that special speech and language services can be provided in the regular classroom through the collaborative efforts of speech-language pathologists and regular classroom teachers. In the opening chapters, a brief primer on the speech and language problems which may be encountered among children in regular education classrooms is presented. Remaining chapters offer descriptions of six programs (early intervention-prevention programs, speech deviations programs, and programs for communicative disorders) in the following locations: Mesa, Arizona; Gouldsboro, Maine; Seattle, Washington; Amherst, Massachusetts; St. Louis, Missouri; and Greensboro, North Carolina. Appended are a list of representative speech and language tests and a list of related publications.

266. Teacher Education: Renegotiating Roles for Mainstreaming. Grosenick, Judith K.; Reynolds, Maynard C., Council for Exceptional Children, Reston, VA; Minnesota University, Minneapolis, National Support Systems Project, 1978, 389p. Sponsoring agency: Bureau of Education for the Handicapped (DHEW/OE), Washington, DC, Division of Personnel Preparation (ED 159 156; Reprint: EDRS; also available from The Council for Exceptional Children, 1920 Association Drive, Reston, VA 22091).

The focus of this volume is upon the changes that are needed in teacher education programs to address the process of mainstreaming handicapped children. The authors of the papers presented are associated with Deans' Grants Projects. The first section presents an overview of past and present special education services and advances a philosophy for the future of teacher education in general. In the second section, the papers examine strategies for change and their application to Deans' Grants Projects. The third section presents case studies of the evolution of three Deans' Grants Projects. The fourth section deals with specific project practices that may hold promise for the successful implementation of change in higher education. The fifth section examines several topics that intersect with the foci of all Deans' Grants Projects. Sections six and seven consist of one paper each. In the former, the author presents a commentary on the challenges facing education in general in today's society; in the latter, there is presented initially an historical analysis of different approaches to serving children with special needs and, then, a synthesis of the efforts, problems, and implications of the Deans' Grants Projects to date.

BOOKS

267 Early Intervention and the Integration of Handicapped and Nonhandicapped Children. Guralnick, Michael J. Baltimore, MD: University Park Press, 1978, 302p.

This collection of 11 articles focuses on integrating handicapped and nonhandicapped children in preschool programs. Article 1 presents arguments for preschool integration. Article 2 discusses research on peer interaction and mixed-age socialization. Article 3 advocates a behavior analysis and operant conditioning approach to studying and influencing peer interactions. In Article 4, four preschool model programs—behavioral, normal developmental, cognitive developmental, and cognitive learning—are described. Article 5 specifies dimensions of integrated preschool programs which promote development of handicapped children. In Article 6, the feasibility of training young delayed children to imitate behavior of nondelayed classmates is discussed. Article 7 reports studies of an integrated, cognitively oriented preschool program. Article 8 reports on integration in a day care center. Article 9 discusses integrating the hearing-impaired child. In Article 10, the mainstreaming of handicapped preschool and kindergarten-age children into open structure classrooms is described. Article 11 describes the merger of a mental retardation agency's early education services with community preschool programs.

268. Mainstreaming Emotionally Disturbed Children. Pappanikou, A. J.; Paul, James L. Syracuse, NY: Syracuse University Press, 1977, 139p.

The nine essays in this volume conceptualize a number of theoretical positions which are vital to implementing a mainstreaming program for emotionally disturbed children. Considered are psychological, legal, and interpersonal factors; the orchestration of success through behavior modification; and implications for leadership and teacher training.

Student Placement: Determining the Least Restrictive Environment

JOURNAL ARTICLES

269. Adapt the Program to Fit the Needs: A Conversation with Kenneth E. Wyatt about the Least Restrictive Environment for Mentally Retarded Students. Thomas, M. Angele. *Education and Training of the Mentally Retarded*. v14, n3, p191–97, Oct 1979.

Service providers to mentally retarded individuals need to be particularly aware of the many factors that impact upon a learning environment, making it more or less restrictive. Because the mentally retarded have inherited a history of isolation and segregation, a child's placement is often equated with environment. Dr. Kenneth E. Wyatt, President of the Council for Exceptional Children, discusses this and other components that must be considered in determining the most appropriate and least restrictive alternatives for educating mentally retarded individuals.

270. Are Profoundly and Severely Retarded People Given Access to the Least Restrictive Environment? An Analysis of One State's Compliance. Miller, Sidney R. et al. *Mental Retardation*. v16, n2, p123–26, Apr 1978.

Primarily in the last decade, a large number of court decisions and federal guidelines have sought to provide retarded persons access to the least restrictive treatment environment. Responses to a set of nine questions asked of several mental health facilities in Illinois indicated that (a) placement staffings are appropriately conducted, (b) parents abrogate their right to monitor their children's services and placements, (c) a small percentage of students who could be placed in less restrictive environments are so placed, and (d) public schools resist placement of the severely or profoundly retarded student.

271. Attitudes of Parents of Mentally-Retarded Children toward Normalization Activities. Ferrara, Dianne Manfredini. *American Journal of Mental Deficiency*. v84, n2, p145–51, Sep 1979.

Parents of educable (EMR) and trainable (TMR) mentally retarded children were surveyed via a five-point Likert scale to determine their attitudes toward normalization activities in general and in relation to their child. Results indicated significant differences in response, with the more positive attitudes being those associated with a general (the mentally retarded population) rather than specific (my child) referent. Within the general-referent group, parents of TMR children displayed the most positive attitudes. Age, sex, and level of retardation had no effect on child-specific responses.

272. Clinical Criteria for Mainstreaming Mildly Handicapped Children. Forness, Steven R. *Psychology in the Schools*. v16, n4, p508–13, Oct 1979 (EJ 210 651; Reprint: UMI).

Although integrating handicapped children into regular classrooms has become well established educational practice, clinical decisions to mainstream a given child should be based on systematic consideration of several factors. These eight criteria are discussed.

273. Criteria for Mainstreaming the Learning Disabled Child into the Regular Classroom. Wilkes, Holly H. et al. *Journal of Learning Disabilities*. v12, n4, p251–56, Apr 1979.

School psychologists (30 Ss), learning disabilities teachers (51 Ss), regular class teachers (33 Ss), and learning disabilities supervisors (16 Ss), were asked to rate the importance of 41 criteria for determining a learning disabled child's readiness for mainstreaming.

274. Do Students Sink or Swim in the Mainstream? Stroud, Marion B. *Phi Delta Kappan*. v60, n4, p316, Dec 1978 (EJ 192 396; Reprint: UMI).

An Ohio study showed that, while the special class generally provided a more positive classroom climate for the handicapped, special classes and regular classes were more alike than they were different.

275. The Education of Severely and Profoundly Retarded Children: Are We Sacrificing the Child to the Concept? Burton, Thomas A.; Hirshoren, Alfred. *Exceptional Children*. v45, n8, p598–602, May 1979.

The authors consider the implementation of P.L. 94-142 (the Education for All Handicapped Children Act) as it relates to educational programing for the severely and profoundly retarded. Their position focuses on three basic issues involving anticipated levels of learning, personnel training, and the appropriate locus of educational services.

276. Integrating the Physically Handicapped Child. Bleck, Eugene E. *Journal of School Health*. v49, n3, p141–46, Mar 1979 (EJ 208 671; Reprint: UMI).

The problems of integrating the physically handicapped child are discussed including descriptions of major handicapping conditions, the development of mainstreaming programs, suggestions for successful programs, and comments on the financial implications of mainstreaming.

277. Inviting Malpractice through Mainstreaming. Dunn, Rita S.; Cole, Robert W. *Educational Leadership*. v36, n5, p302–06, Feb 1979 (EJ 196 158; Reprint: UMI).

Mainstreaming handicapped students without providing adequately for their special needs is malpractice and may lead to litigation.

278. The Least Restrictive Environment. Nix, Gary W. *Volta Review*. v79, n5, p287–96, Sep 1977.

The concept of the least restrictive environment for hearing impaired children is viewed in terms of legal implementation, organizational viewpoints, and procedures for determining the least restrictive environment.

279. The Least Restrictive Environment: Implications for Early Childhood Education. Allen, K. Eileen. *Educational Horizons*. v56, n1, p34–41, Fall 1977 (EJ 174 975; Reprint: UMI).

Suggests that children need the "least restrictive environment" in order for them to learn effectively and develops this concept, embodied in P.L. 94-142, the Education for All Handicapped Children Act. Also discusses the teacher's role in making certain that physical space is planned to stimulate learning.

280. Least-Restrictive Placement: Administrative Wishful Thinking. Cruickshank, William M. *Journal of Learning Disabilities*. v10, n4, p193–94, Apr 1977.

The guest editorial by W. Cruickshank criticizes as facile the assumption that the least restrictive environment for learning disabled children is a regular classroom.

281. Mainstream Placement Question/Check List. Nix, Gary W. *Volta Review*. v79, n5, p345–46, Sep 1977.

Presented is a checklist of child, placement situation, and family parameters which contribute to successful mainstream placement for hearing impaired students.

282. Mainstreamed vs. Self-Contained Classes: A Two-Year Study of Their Effects on the Personal Adjustment and Academic Achievement of Children with Learning Disabilities. Schiff, Gloria et al. *Education*. v99, n4, p397–405, Sum 1979 (EJ 206 934; Reprint: UMI).

Sixteen of 33 learning disabled students, all of whom had spent a year in self-contained classrooms, were placed in a mainstream class for the 1976-77 year. Ratings of personal, social, and academic adjustment and achievement test scores indicated that the self-contained classroom environment produced more positive adjustment.

283. Mainstreaming Characteristics of Orthopedically Handicapped Students in California. Best, Gary A. *Rehabilitation Literature*. v38, n6–7, p205–09, Jun–Jul 1977.

Surveys about mainstreaming orthopedically handicapped students were completed by 74 school administrators in California. Topics covered included an operational definition of mainstreaming; an identification of children by grade level and disability type; criteria for the selection of children and the role of teachers, administrators, and parents in decisionmaking regarding placements; and the training of personnel for successful implementation of the placement.

284. Mainstreaming Current Flows Two Ways. Houck, Cherry; Sherman, Ann. *Academic Therapy*. v15, n2, p133–40, Nov 1979.

The authors examine the mainstreaming concept, its rationale, and considerations for successful implementation. They present cost comparison and achievement effectiveness data for regular, resource, and special class programs for moderately to severely learning disabled children.

285. Mainstreaming EMR Students at Secondary Level: A Consideration of the Issues. Powers, David A. *High School Journal*. v63, n3, p102–08, Dec 1979.

This article lists current objections to mainstreaming at the secondary level: lack of empirical support for the concept, inappropriate curriculum, lack of support personnel, negative teacher attitudes, lack of program flexibility, and the impossibility of individualized instruction. Each objection is considered and change strategies suggested.

286. Mainstreaming the LD Child: A Cautionary Note. Decker, Robert J.; Decker, Lawrence A. *Academic Therapy*. v12, n3, p353–56, Spr 1977 (EJ 167 922; Reprint: UMI).

Among six reasons cited for advocating caution in mainstreaming learning disabled students are lowered self-concepts in mainstreamed students due to competition with their normal peers, lack of individual attention, and inadequate teacher preparation.

287. Mainstreaming vs. the Special Setting. Hannah, Elaine P.; Parker, Ronald M. *Academic Therapy*. v15, n3, p271–78, Jan 1980.

Discusses academic, environmental, psychosocial, and personal factors to consider in the decision to maintain a learning disabled child in the regular classroom or move that child to a special class.

288. Mainstreaming Young Emotionally Disturbed Children: Rationale and Restraints. Meisels, Samuel J.; Friedland, Seymour J. *Behavioral Disorders*. v3, n3, p178–85, May 1978.

The article examines some of the unique issues involved in mainstreaming preschool and kindergarten emotionally disturbed children.

289. Maintaining the Mainstreamed Child in the Regular Classroom: The Decision-Making Process. Heron, Timothy E. *Journal of Learning Disabilities*. v11, n4, p210–16, Apr 1978.

Described is a composite decision-making approach for maintaining a mainstreamed child in the regular classroom.

290. On a Distinction between the Education of the Severely and Profoundly Handicapped and a Doctrine of Limitations. Sontage, Ed. et al. *Exceptional Children*. v45, n8, p605–16, May 1979.

The authors respond to T. Burton and A. Hirshoren's position regarding the three areas of the education of the severely and profoundly retarded: (1) anticipated levels of learning, (2) personnel training, and (3) locus of educational services.

291. Politics, Litigation, and Mainstreaming: Special Education's Demise? Bartlett, Richard H. *Mental Retardation*. v15, n1, p24–26, Feb 1977.

In the name of nondiscrimination and civil rights, special education is being challenged to develop alternative strategies that may lead to its own demise. But if we consider the development of the self-image, self-control, academic success, and independence as the benchmarks of the educational process, the present literature suggests that special education must remain for some mentally retarded students, who would suffer social rejection in a regular classroom.

292. The Principal and Special Education Placement. Yoshida, Roland K. et al. *National Elementary Principal*. v58, n1, p34–38, Oct 1978 (EJ 196 127; Reprint: UMI).

Uses the placement practices of one school as a base for discussing placement practices and due process required under the regulations for Public Law 94-142.

293. Reservations about the Effect of PL 94-142 on the Education of Visually Handicapped Children. Hapeman, Lawrence. *Education of the Visually Handicapped*. v9, n2, p33–36, Sum 1977.

The author cites reasons to believe that implementation of P.L. 94-142 may be detrimental to the education of visually impaired children. The suggestion is made that heavy emphasis on "appropriate" as opposed to "optimum" educational services could result in reduction, rather than improvement, in quality of programs if the result is increased avoidance of employment of residential schools as an integral part of the system.

294. Surviving in the Regular Classroom: A Follow-Up of Mainstreamed Children with Learning Disabilities. Ritter, David R. *Journal of School Psychology*. v16, n3, p253–56, Fall 1978 (EJ 188 395; Reprint: UMI).

Twenty elementary-age children diagnosed as learning disabled were assessed. It was concluded that regular classroom instruction alone may be insufficient for mainstreamed children with learning disabilities and that supplemental programming seems necessary if prior rates of academic learning are to be maintained.

295. Teaching Learning and Behavioral Disabled Students in Least Restrictive Environments. Stephens, Thomas M. *Behavioral Disorders*. v2, n3, p146–51, May 1977.

The placement of learning disabled and behaviorally disordered children in the least restrictive setting requires consideration of both environmental conditions and psychological factors which contribute to the handicap.

296. Toward the Realization of the Least Restrictive Educational Environments for Severely Handicapped Students. Brown, Lou et al. *AAESPH Review*. v2, n4, p195–202, Dec 1977.

This paper discusses least restrictive educational environments in relation to segregation versus integration, interactions with nonhandicapped age peers, the ratio between handicapped and nonhandicapped students, chronologically age-appropriate educational environments, architectural barriers and prosthetized environments, "normal" organization of the school day, equal access to school facilities and resources, transportation, and ancillary services. The fundamental premise offered here is that educational service delivery models for severely handicapped students must closely approximate the best educational service delivery models used for nonhandicapped students.

297. When Is a Child Ready for Mainstreaming? *Exceptional Parent*. v9, n5, pR2–R8, Oct 1979.

Several educators and parents of handicapped children respond to this question, citing criteria for determining the readiness of the disabled child and of the school itself for mainstreaming.

REPORTS

298. Beyond the Early Identification and Treatment of the Young Child: The Chronic Child Patient. Silverman, Morton. 1978, 14p (ED 162 484; Reprint: EDRS).

Examples of three emotionally disturbed children whose behavior deteriorated in regular class placements are cited to support the author's contention that the least restrictive environment principle may err in the direction of underserving and underprotecting handicapped children. Also questioned is the violation of individual differences by legislation such as P.L. 94-142, the Education for All Handicapped Children, if normalcy is the espoused goal.

299. Comparing Professional and Parent Criteria for Placement of the Severely Handicapped in Segregated and Regular School-Based Programs.* Calvin, Howard T., Indiana University, 1977, 150p (7801007; Reprint: DC).

This research undertook to identify and compare the criteria by which parents and professionals determine the most appropriate type of public school program and facility to serve the severely handicapped of their community.

A video-taped debate involving parents of handicapped students and experts in the education and training of the severely handicapped formed the study's principal stimulus. It was used to determine whether subjects—parents of handicapped and nonhandicapped children, regular and special education teachers, and regular and special education administrators—should emerge with altered opinions from viewing the taped presentation and participating in group discussion of issues salient in the debate.

The study surveyed two separate communities, each of which was examining the feasibility of building a segregated special school for their severely handicapped students. At the investigator's request, the director of special education at each experimental site invited individuals to participate. The 118 experimental subjects completed a Likert-type survey instrument before and after the presentation and discussion of the video-taped debate. The study also used a comparison group from each site; these 73 comparison subjects completed the survey instrument only once and did not see the debate or discuss it.

Examination of data revealed that, on the pretest, 49 percent of the experimental subjects sampled in Illinois believed that severely handicapped students should be placed in a segregated special school; their posttest scores showed that 76 percent favored a special school setting. In Indiana, viewing and discussing the debate did not significantly influence the experimental subjects. There were no significant differences between the responses of experimental and comparison groups. Posttest scores indicated that, at both sites, all six subgroups agreed upon the segregated special school as the setting most appropriate to education and training of the severely handicapped.

300. The Effects of Mainstreaming and Self-Contained Education for Hearing Impaired Students. Risley, Gary W., Los Altos School District, CA, Aug 1977, 181p. Sponsorng agency: California State Department of Education, Sacramento (ED 150 762; Reprint: EDRS).

Compared with 14 hearing impaired students (grades 4-9) in either integrated or self-contained classes were student achievement and social development, teacher variables, and parental understanding and expectations. Ss' cumulative records were used to obtain IQ and achievement data; Ss were given a self-concept rating scale; parents and teachers were also given attitude scales; and structured interviews were conducted with students, parents, teachers, and administrators in both programs. Few significant differences in self-concept were found between Ss in the two programs. Parents of integrated students were more likely than parents of self-contained students to report there was ''no chance at all'' that their child would have more deaf than hearing friends as an adult. Structured interview data yielded significant differences among parents of both groups in such areas as confidence in program, knowledge of handicaps, exposure to hearing impaired literature, membership in associations for parents of hearing impaired Ss, and use of sign language. Results were related to how decisions to participate in either type of program are made and to the structure and functioning of each program.

301. Formulating Intervention Strategies to Maintain the Mildly Handicapped Student in the Regular Classroom. Pollock, Nancy; Taylor, Marjane. Apr 1977, 22p; Paper presented at the Annual International Convention, The Council for Exceptional Children (55th, Atlanta, GA, April 11–15, 1977) (ED 139 155; Reprint: EDRS).

Provided in three sections is a presentation on providing services to identify, assess, and develop intervention strategies for mildly handicapped students in the regular classroom. Section I provides a definition of an educational strategist, and background information on the referral system and program in Iowa. Covered in Section II are the people a diagnostician may want to talk to when processing a referral, the information gathering process, areas to consider when analyzing a student's difficulties, and suggestions (such as prompting, grouping within the classroom, and taping reading assignments and tests) requiring minimal modification of the standard classroom program. A third section contains two brief case studies. A sample prereferral screening data sheet is appended.

302. How to Select the Least Restrictive, but Most Appropriate, Educational Program for Handicapped Children. Brown, Craig S. Apr 1977, 9p; Paper presented at the Annual International Convention, The Council for Exceptional Children (55th, Atlanta, GA, April 11–15, 1977) (ED 139 165; Reprint: EDRS).

Described are the procedures for a referral-to-placement process which places each handicapped child in the least restrictive, most appropriate, educational program. The process stresses the role of the regular education teacher in determining the special education program options appropriate for the student. A sample report prepared by a regular education teacher is included.

303. Least Restrictive Educational Environment/Pupil Match. Merz, William R.; Raske, David E. Aug 1978, 110p; best copy available. Sponsoring agency: California State Department of Education, Sacramento (ED 163 667; Reprint: EDRS—HC not available).

A study was made to identify and define a variety of educational placement alternatives with reference to the concept of restrictiveness and to match these educational settings with the cognitive, affective, and physical development of exceptional pupils. A profile of pupil characteristics was derived and validated on approximately 200 special education pupils placed in least restrictive environments in California. The efficacy of their functioning in those environments was evaluated. Based on the

study results, a system was devised for predicting program membership, to obtain a set of possible least restrictive placements for a handicapped student.

304. Mainstreaming the Hearing-Impaired Child: Process Not Goal. Ewoldt, Carolyn. 1979, 14p (ED 168 275; Reprint: EDRS).

Issues involved in mainstreaming deaf and hearing impaired students are examined. The child's acceptance by hearing peers, possible psychological immaturity, controversies over manual communication and oral language, and factors affecting student placement are among the issues explored. Suggestions are given for classroom teachers working with mainstreamed hearing impaired students.

305. Parent Perceptions of Least Restrictive Alternative.* Yeager, Bruce G., The University of Toledo, 1979, 111p (8002827; Reprint: DC).

The purpose of this study was to determine parent perceptions of least restrictive alternative placement for their children in the Lucas County Program for the Mentally Retarded. A random sample of parents was selected from the population of parents within the entire Lucas County Program to receive a parent questionnaire. The sample included 191 families all located within the geographical boundaries of Lucas County, Ohio. One hundred fifty-four questionnaires were returned for analysis which yielded a rate of return of 81 percent.

The majority of respondents were mothers with children in the school program of the Lucas County Program for the Mentally Retarded. The greater part were also members of the Lucas County Association for Retarded Citizens.

Most respondents had been involved in the program for 10 years or more with a mean age of 47 for parents and 18 for their children.

The conclusion was reached that respondents were not in favor of mainstreaming their children into public school and felt that the present, out-of-school placement of their children was the least restrictive alternative for them.

306. The Principle of the Least Restrictive Environment and the Schools. Brinegar, Leslie. Mar 1978, 13p (ED 162 445; Reprint: EDRS).

Issues concerning the interpretation and application of the least restrictive environment (LRE) principle for handicapped children are examined. Overly optimistic predictions about the use of regular class placements for all exceptional children are cautioned against, and issues regarding LRE in private schools and separate segregated public schools are examined. California policy and regulations are cited.

307. Reintegration of Emotionally Disabled Pupils. Iowa Study: Preliminary Report. Smith, Carl R. et al., Iowa State Department of Public Instruction, Des Moines, Division of Special Education, Jan 1979, 50p (ED 176 439; Reprint: EDRS).

To determine how many emotionally disturbed (ED) Iowa students were reintegrated into regular classrooms, by what criteria, and by whom, a study of ED teachers from 76 public school programs serving this population was undertaken. Results of the questionnaire showed that 85.5 percent of respondents worked in school districts with over 3,000 students, 76.4 percent had been teaching 3 years or less, 67.1 percent worked in self-contained (or self-contained, severe) classrooms, and the majority of students were in elementary school. Other findings revealed that 84.2 percent of the respondents indicated that no students had been referred to a less restrictive ED programing during the 1977-78 school year, and that the likelihood of a particular pupil being integrated decreases in relation to the length of time the pupil has been in the ED program. It was shown that readiness of a student to return to a regular classroom rests with the perceptions of the individual ED teacher regarding the student's progress and that 65.5 percent of the respondents felt that integration procedures were not clearly defined. In selecting the regular classroom or teacher to be involved in the integration process most respondents indicated that humane, attitudinal, and personality factors were more highly valued than knowledge of educational techniques or educational philosophies. The teacher questionnaire is appended.

308. Service Provider Agreement and Special Education Reform.* Flor, John Fulton, University of Pennsylvania, 1978, 236p (7908734; Reprint: DC).

This study investigates the capacity of service providers for independently agreeing on special educational programming for particular educably retarded children ages 8 to 11.

The study was conducted in Delaware County, Pennsylvania. A questionnaire was developed after interviewing 24 professionals, visiting three classrooms and examining the program plans for 40 students. The 42-item questionnaire taps realistic decision making in such areas as diagnosis, educational placement, teaching priorities, and intervention techniques for personal adjustment problems. According to the interviewees, responses on it, taken together, adequately reflect the permutation of programming for EMR children within the Intermediate Unit being studied. Twenty-one professionals including a psychologist, a teacher, and an administrator in each of seven school districts were given three in-depth anonymous case studies which were developed from the files of three actual children. Each professional completed a questionnaire for each of the three cases.

Levels of calculated agreement among professionals were consistently poor whether the reference group was the total 21 raters, the three professional subgroups or the three-member teams. Analysis by individual cases yielded agreements averaging approximately 30 percent on scales guaranteeing at least 10 percent. Across case computations revealed agreement percentages which were, more often than not, lower than would be expected by a chance assignment of ratings.

The findings suggest that service providers, within the Intermediate Unit, were not able to agree on "appropriate" programming. Since congruence was assumed to be a necessary condition for fulfillment of "appropriateness," the success of current reforms is called into question. Additional observations about the accomplishments and failures of the first year of P.L. 94-142 are offered.

309. Who Are the Deaf Children in "Mainstream" Programs? Research Bulletin: Series R, No. 4. Karchmer, Michael A.; Trybus, Raymond J., Gallaudet College, Washington, DC, Office of Demographic Studies, Oct 1977, 12p; Paper presented at the Convention of American Instructors of the Deaf (48th, Los Angeles, CA, June, 1977) (ED 148 073; Reprint: EDRS).

The paper examines the extent of integrated placement (mainstreaming) of hearing impaired children in the United States and describes a variety of educationally salient characteristics of these students. As compared with hearing impaired children in other types of educational programs, students in integrated programs are reported to have significantly less severe hearing loss, higher family incomes, and other distinctive characteristics. It is noted that programs are presently serving a group of hearing impaired children who are very different on many educationally critical dimensions from those children who attend other types of special education programs.

MAKING MAINSTREAMING WORK

Handbooks, Guidelines, and Resources

JOURNAL ARTICLES

310. Accommodating Learning Disabilities: Creating the Least Restrictive Environment. Lockwood, Ann Vevier. *Illinois Schools Journal.* v58, n4, p33–36, Win 1978–79 (EJ 200 648; Reprint: UMI).

Presented in this article are various strategies for integrating learning disabled children into academic programs. Suggestions are made in the areas of mathematics, classroom environment, social studies, and science.

311. Active Academic Games: The Aim of the Game is Mainstreaming. Salend, Spencer J. *Teaching Exceptional Children.* v12, n1, p3–6, Fall 1979.

Academic games that allow for group interactions, individualized curricula controlled by the teacher, and multiple entry points for children functioning at different levels, can aid in making the mainstreamed classroom a prosthetic environment. The purpose of this article is to provide teachers with a model for developing academic games to help implement mainstreaming.

312. Autistic Children in School. Dunlap, Glen et al. *Exceptional Children.* v45, n7, p552–58, Apr 1979.

A brief description of autism is presented, along with evidence documenting the educability of autistic children. Some issues relating to autistic children's behavior are described, and teacher and administrator preparation is reviewed.

313. Beyond the IEP: A Task Analysis of the Reading Process. Morsink, Catherine. *Education Unlimited.* v1, n1, p37–42, Apr 1979.

Using word attack reading skills as an example, the article focuses on a process for translating the IEP (individualized education program) into a guide for effective instructional planning with handicapped students.

314. Books Can Introduce Your Class to the Mainstreamed Child. Putnam, Rosemary W. *Learning.* v7, n2, p118–20, Oct 1978 (EJ 197 199; Reprint: UMI).

A list of books dealing with handicapped children is provided for reading by children in a regular classroom to help them understand and accept their handicapped peers.

315. Consulting with Teachers of Handicapped Children in the Mainstream. Westling, David L.; Joiner, M. Douglas. *Elementary School Guidance and Counseling.* v13, n3, p207–13, Feb 1979 (EJ 197 552; Reprint: UMI).

Suggests useful approaches for school counselors to use when consulting with teachers who are attempting to create least restrictive environments for handicapped children.

316. Counseling with Handicapped Children. DeBlassie, Richard R.; Lebsock, Marjean Spayer. *Elementary School Guidance and Counseling.* v13, n3, p199–206, Feb 1979 (EJ 197 551; Reprint: UMI).

The characteristics of such high incidence handicaps as educable mental retardation, learning disabilities, behavior disorders/emotional disturbances are described. Special considerations for counseling handicapped children, as well as strategies and techniques for individual and group counseling, are also discussed.

317. Developing Acceptance toward the Handicapped. McKalip, Keith J. *School Counselor.* v26, n5, p293–98, May 1979 (EJ 204 220; Reprint: UMI).

Presents an approach to developing acceptance of handicapped students in a mainstreaming situation by staff and normal students. Planning should be developed prior to the handicapped child's entrance into a regular classroom. Handicapped learner labels should be avoided. Counselors should provide leadership in this endeavor.

318. Developing IEP's for Physically Handicapped Students: A Transdisciplinary Viewpoint. Sirvis, Barbara. *Teaching Exceptional Children.* v10, n3, p78–82, Spr 1978.

The article reviews curriculum areas, team roles and approaches, and the transdisciplinary approach in developing individualized education programs for physically handicapped students.

319. ERIC/RCS: Mainstreaming and Reading Instruction. Rupley, William H.; Blair, Timothy R. *Reading Teacher*. v32, n6, p762–65, Mar 1979 (EJ 202 897; Reprint: UMI).

Discusses documents found in the ERIC system that deal specifically with research, curriculum guides, and model programs related to reading instruction and mainstreaming.

320. Finding the Right Environment for Handicapped Students. Hedberg, Sally. *Thrust for Educational Leadership*. v9, n2, p4–5, Nov 1979 (EJ 213 728; Reprint: UMI).

A few tips for helping students who are designated as disabled integrate into the regular school setting socially as well as academically are offered to administrators and teachers.

321. Getting Handicapped Students into Regular Classrooms. Moore, Carm. *Thrust for Educational Leadership*. v9, n2, p18–19, Nov 1979 (EJ 213 735; Reprint: UMI).

Presented is a brief framework, with suggestions to help a principal provide staff assistance where necessary when implementing a mainstreaming effort.

322. A Handicapped Kid in My Class? Leone, Peter; Retish, Paul. *Social Studies*. v69, n1, p18–20, Jan–Feb 1978 (EJ 176 389; Reprint: UMI).

Suggests adaptations of curriculum and awareness activities for students to prepare for the arrival of handicapped students who are to be mainstreamed into the general public school environment.

323. Have Questions about Mainstreaming? These Groups Are Ready to Help You Find the Answers. *Instructor*. v87, n6, p132–134, Jan 1978 (EJ 174 052; Reprint: UMI).

Presents a current annotated list of more than 25 national nonprofit groups that can help answer questions about mainstreaming of children with various special needs.

324. Helping the Special Student Fit In. Bybee, Rodger W. *Science Teacher*. v46, n7, p22–24, Oct 1979 (EJ 210 157; Reprint: UMI).

Guidelines are presented to help the classroom teacher effectively deal with handicapped students. Included are general guidelines and suggestions specific to hearing impaired, visually handicapped, physically handicapped, speech and language impaired, learning disabled, mentally retarded, emotionally disturbed, and disruptive students.

325. The Language-Delayed Child in the Mainstreamed Primary Classroom. Scofield, Sandra J. *Language Arts*. v55, n6, p719–23, 732, Sep 1978 (EJ 188 535; Reprint: UMI).

Language delayed children need systematic instruction, experience with a range of language functions, and opportunities for spontaneous speech.

326. The Law and Children's Literature. Hornburger, Jane M.; Shapiro, Phyllis P. *Teacher Educator*. v12, n4, p28–34, Spr 1977.

Reading materials for the mentally and/or physically handicapped child are suggested to aid the classroom teacher in assimilating the exceptional child into the mainstream classroom. Books about children with various handicaps are listed.

327. Mainstreaming: Who? What? When? Where? Why? Moller, Barbara. *Early Years*. v9, n3, p48–50, Nov 1978 (available from Allen Raymond, Inc., P.O. Box 1223, Darien, CT 06820).

This article addresses many questions on mainstreaming for the regular class teacher: Who will be the handicapped child's friend? Who is available to provide services? What should be done about a childs academic or social problems in class? When should reports, referrals, and conferences be made? Where can information be gained and problems reported? Why is mainstreaming important?

328. Mainstreaming a Child with Spina Bifida. Nelson, Dorothy H. *Instruction*. v88, n8, p134–36, Mar 1979 (EJ 199 926; Reprint: UMI).

In discussing the case of one six-year-old boy, the author describes the nature of spina bifida and some of the adaptations required to mainstream a child with this disability.

329. Mainstreaming Eight Types of Exceptionalities. Powell, Jack V. *Education*. v99, n1, p55–58, Fall 1978 (EJ 192 953; Reprint: UMI).

Presenting provisions for mainstreaming eight types of exceptionalities, this article includes a chart which provides suggestions regarding physical surroundings, instructional activities, materials, teaching strategies, and meeting emotional/social needs for the following: educable mentally retarded; speech disabilities; behavioral disabilities; cripple/health impaired; general learning disabilities; hearing; visual; and gifted.

330. Mainstreaming in Early Childhood. Strategies and Resources.† McLoughlin, James A.; Kershman, Susan M. *Young Children*. v34, n4, p54–66, May 1979.

The article focuses on strategies and resources available for the mainstreaming of young handicapped children. Suggestions for staff training and a bibliography of seven training materials are provided along with a list of organizations that have information on recent legislation, legal rights, and strategies for parents in working with their handicapped children. The identification process is outlined and a table of screening and assessment instruments is included. Information on materials and methods for teaching the young handicapped child is identified and basic skill areas and materials/books for teaching are listed. Addresses of publishers of six guides in the selection of equipment and materials for early childhood programs are provided.

331. Mainstreaming That Works in Elementary and Secondary Schools. Birch, Jack W. *Journal of Teacher Education*. v29, n6, p18–21, Nov–Dec 1978 (EJ 193 339; Reprint: UMI).

Prototypes of successful mainstreaming programs are described and suggestions about sound mainstreaming practices are made for school systems beginning this program.

332. Medical Considerations for Multiple-Handicapped Children in the Public Schools. Bryan, Elizabeth et al. *Journal of School Health*. v48, n2, p84–89, Feb 1978.

The authors discuss concerns and practical suggestions involved in the education of multiply handicapped children in the following problem areas: first aid, emergency care, and disaster planning; sanitation; environment; safety in routine and supplemental activities; therapy procedures; and staff protection, training, orientation, and special qualifications.

333. New Ways to Handle Old Problems. Lovitt, Tom. *Early Years*. v9, n8, p34–36, Apr 1979 (available from Allen Raymond, Inc., P.O. Box 1223, Darien, CT 06820).

The author discusses methods for managing feisty or nonmotivated mainstreamed students. Both old-fashioned punishments and modern reinforcers are discussed.

334. Put On a Handicap. Huttar, Ethel. *Early Years*. v8, n8, p46–49, Apr 1978 (available from Allen Raymond, Inc., P.O. Box 1223, Darien, CT 06820).

Suggests songs, children's books, and role playing activities to prepare nonhandicapped kindergartners for mainstreaming.

335. Putting Out the Welcome Mat. Glazzard, Peggy. *Early Years*. v7, n9, p41–43, 65, May 1977 (available from Allen Raymond, Inc., P.O. Box 1223, Darien, CT 06820).

Suggests ways a classroom teacher can prepare students for mainstreaming and adapt teaching methods and materials to the special child.

336. Recommended Resources. Redden, Martha Ross. *New Directions for Higher Education; No. 25 (Assuring Access for the Handicapped)*. v7, n1, p113–17, 1979 (EJ 205 019; Reprint: UMI).

References to other publications point to useful sources of information and advice for college administrators and faculty leaders seeking to assure access for the handicapped. Knowledgeable people, organizations, local and state laws, and national resources are the major sources of information noted.

337. Removing Restrictions from the Least Restrictive Environment. Walberg, Franette Adair. *Thrust for Educational Leadership*. v9, n2, p6–8, Nov 1979 (EJ 213 729; Reprint: UMI).

The author suggests ways to teach "campus survival skills" to handicapped students, and suggests techniques for successfully integrating these students into the mainstream of campus life.

338. Science and the Physically Handicapped. Ricker, Kenneth S. *Viewpoints in Teaching and Learning*. v55, n1, p67–76, Win 1979 (EJ 205 579; Reprint: UMI).

The integration of physically (sensory and orthopedic) handicapped students into science classes creates a complex problem for science educators. Suggestions are offered for teacher preparation and for the development of specialized materials and modifications for instructional strategies.

339. Section 504: Confusion and Controversy. *American School and University*. v50, n1, p33, Sep 1977 (EJ 165 852; Reprint: UMI).

The Architectural and Transportation Barriers Compliance Board has published a book of technical guidelines for barrier-free architecture that includes policy statements and their rationale, measured drawings, and specific directives.

340. Sighted Children Learn about Blindness. Scheffers, Wenda L. *Journal of Visual Impairment and Blindness*. v71, n6, p258–61, Jun 1977.

In a 20-lesson unit, sighted second- to fourth-grade students were taught about the long cane, guide dogs, daily living skills, eye physiology, causes of blindness, eye care, braille, and attitudes toward blindness.

341. Special Touches. Glazzard, Peggy. *Early Years*. v8, n8, p50–52, Apr 1978 (available from Allen Raymond, Inc., P.O. Box 1223, Darien, CT 06820).

Suggests ways to simulate handicaps (earplugs, blindfolds, reverse writing, etc) to sensitize nonhandicapped youngsters to the problems faced by their handicapped peers.

342. Teaching the Behavior Disordered Child. Neel, Richard S. *Early Years*. v9, n8, p27–30, Apr 1979 (available from Allen Raymond, Inc., P.O. Box 1223, Darien, CT 06820).

Techniques are suggested to classroom teachers for coping with children who demonstrate overactive, bizarre, or aggressive behaviors. Identifying problems, allowing for emotional release, and applying "natural consequences" discipline are discussed.

343. There's a Deaf Child in My Class. Culhan, Barry R.; Curwin, Richard. *Learning*. v7, n2, p111–12, 117, Oct 1978 (EJ 197 197; Reprint: UMI).

Specific suggestions are made to help a teacher communicate successfully with a deaf child.

344. Visually Handicapped Children in the Regular Classroom. Scholl, Geraldine T. *Teacher*. v95, n6, p79–80, Feb 1978 (EJ 182 635; Reprint: UMI).

Public Law 94-142 emphasizes the least restrictive environment and an individualized educational program (IEP) based on diagnosed needs for handicapped students. However, successful mainstreaming (regular class placement) of visually handicapped children involves many resources. Describes teacher role and what can be done in adjusting handicapped students to a normal classroom environment.

REPORTS

345. Administrators Resource Manual for the Deinstitutionalization of Children and Youth. Southwest Regional Resource Center, Salt Lake City, UT, Jan 1979, 207p. Sponsoring agency: Bureau of Education for the Handicapped (DHEW/OE), Washington, DC (ED 168 252; Reprint: EDRS).

Designed to help administrators involved with the deinstitutionalization of Arizona's severely and profoundly handicapped children, the manual details cooperative planning decisions and describes components of the educational program which are different from those previously delivered to less handicapped children. In the first section, responsibility, location of services, and service procurement information is listed for the public schools and the Division of Developmental Disabilities/Mental Retardation. Eleven special considerations for the deinstitutionalized students (including assessment and programing resources, toilet training, transportation, and medical services) are discussed and resources are identified for each area. Three case studies are provided. Among five appendixes is information on placement into services from the community.

346. Aids to Psycholinguistic Teaching for the Regular Class Teacher with Mainstreamed Exceptionals. Lazar, Alfred L. 1977, 89p; Best copy available (ED 150 819; Reprint EDRS—HC not available; also available from PASKT Publications, 100 Via Capay, Palos Verdes Estates, CA 90274).

Intended for the regular class teacher, the booklet contains 72 sample lesson activities for use with mainstreamed learning disabled students. Activities are organized around the Illinois Test of Psycholinguistic Abilities and cover the following areas: auditory reception, visual reception, auditory association, visual association, verbal expression, manual expression, grammatic closure, visual closure, auditory sequential memory, visual sequential memory, auditory closure, and sound blending. Provided for each activity are descriptions of the procedures, materials needed, and evaluation criteria.

347. Billy: The Visually Impaired Child in Your Classroom. Gear, Gayle et al., Alabama University, Birmingham, School of Education, 1979, 28p. Sponsoring agency: Bureau of Education for the Handicapped (DHEW/OE), Washington, DC, Division of Personnel Preparation (ED 176 456; Reprint: EDRS—HC not available; also available from The Interrelated Teacher Education Project, The University of Alabama, Birmingham, AL 35294).

Intended for regular class teachers, the booklet provides information to aid in mainstreaming the visually impaired (VH) child. Sections address the following areas: characteristics of the VH child (legal and educational definitions, common visual defects, etiology); identification and signs of visual problems (warning symptoms); the vision specialist and assessment team; behavior patterns (suggestions for teaching the VH child); and special equipment and resources (writing equipment, mathematics equipment, and audio aids and reading materials).

348. Children with Special Needs in Day Care: A Guide to Integration (A Guide for Integrating Developmentally Delayed Children into Regular Day Care Services). National Institute on Mental Retardation, Toronto, Ontario, 1978, 117p. Sponsoring agency: Canadian Association for the Mentally Retarded, Toronto, Ontario (ED 167 243; Reprint: EDRS).

This handbook (written in English and French) provides guidelines for integrating children with special needs into regular day care programs and discusses the need for a network of social services for these children and their families. The guide explains: (1) the rationale for mainstreaming and the advantages and disadvantages of categorizing special needs; (2) the main components of early developmental programs; (3) different forms mainstreaming can take and the major factors in instituting mainstreaming in a day care facility; and (4) how to structure a program for developmentally delayed children within a regular early childhood service and how to monitor the mainstreaming process. A checklist for assessing the quality of integrated preschool programs is included and examples are given of services (in addition to day care and preschool programs) which would comprise a total network of resources for children with special needs and their families. The guide concludes with a discussion of the directions in which service for handicapped children should go (e.g., inter-agency coordination). A resource section with references to printed and audiovisual materials and an appendix listing Canadian organizations for handicapped persons are included.

349. Considerations in the Integration of Behaviorally Disordered Students into the Regular Classroom: Implications for the School Principal. Oaks, Carol A. et al. Apr 1979, 13p; Paper presented at the Annual International Convention, The Council for Exceptional Children (57th, Dallas, TX, April 22–27, 1979, Session F-68) (ED 171 096; Reprint: EDRS).

The paper describes mainstreaming of behaviorally disordered students at Orange Elementary School (in Waterloo, Iowa). The author, who is principal of the school, makes a number of suggestions for the implementation of mainstreaming, such as being aware of the structural capabilities of the individual school building (a school with many steps, for example, would not easily accommodate physically handicapped children), planning the scheduling of the handicapped children so that they can easily attend mainstreamed classes, and selecting staff (whenever possible) whose attitudes toward the handicapped and working with them are positive. Other suggestions include inservice education and reduction in regular class size (to assist teachers in coping with the extra time involved in mainstream programming). The author explains that mainstreaming should not be attempted all at once; taking time to know each child is important. Enlargement of budgets, student attitudes, and consistent discipline are also explored. Compliance with the law in matters such as securing the proper tests and evaluations, and obtaining signatures from parents and the implications of mainstreaming in negotiations with teachers are reviewed.

350. The Counselor's Role in Individualized Education Program (IEP) Development. Wheaton, Peter J.; Vandergriff, Arvil F. Nov 1978, 22p; Paper presented at the Conference of the Florida Personnel and Guidance Association (29th, Orlando, FL, November 16–18, 1978); some pages will not reproduce well (ED 174 896; Reprint: EDRS).

Training techniques available for school counselors which can be utilized in working with regular classroom teachers, special education teachers, placement committee staffings and in the liaison role currently emerging are described. The materials presented address the following areas of concern: (1) recent trends in special education programming, such as the requirements of Public Law 94-142, which have contributed to a changing counselor role; (2) the challenge of the individualized education program (IEP), which details the unique needs of the handicapped child and is accentuated by the requirement that a group of people develop, implement as well as monitor the program; (3) strategies for effective group problem solving which appear to be the responsibility of the school counselor; and (4) the potential for the counselor's skillfulness in human relations to have a positive effect on a staffing committee's group decision regarding IEPs. The appendices contain the inserts which provide the model and forms for use in developing IEPs.

351. Creating an Accessible Campus. Coons, Maggie; Milner, Margaret, Association of Physical Plant Administrators of Universities and Colleges, Washington, DC, 1978, 151p. Sponsoring agency: EXXON Education Foundation, New York (ED 175 080; Reprint: EDRS—HC not available; also available from American Association of Physical Plant Administrators of Universities and Colleges, Eleven Dupont Circle, Suite 250, Washington, DC 20036).

This book was developed to help administrators meet the challenge of compliance with the regulations implementing Section 504 of the Rehabilitation Act of 1973. All colleges, universities, and other organizations that are funded by the Department of Health, Education, and Welfare (HEW) have until June 3, 1980, to make structural modifications necessary to make their programs fully accessible to handicapped persons. Programs are to be accessible now in all cases in which structural modifications are not necessary. Nine chapters and an introduction trace the steps in developing a program for accessibility, from understanding what constitutes a barrier in the built environment to specific recommendations on site and building design and design of science laboratories. The functional relationships between various disabilities and the use of the environment are described. Design requirements associated with these functional relationships are described and illustrated. State of the art information about instructional aids is broken down into three groups: instructional aids for the mobility impaired, aids for students with sight disabilities, and aids for students with hearing disabilities. The final chapter discusses resource and funding sources.

352. A Directory of Selected Resources in Special Education. Series No. 2. Merrimack Education Center, Chelmsford, MA, 1977, 40p (ED 136 520; Reprint: EDRS).

Intended for teachers and administrators integrating special needs students into appropriate mainstream settings, the directory provides an annotated listing of resources covering home-school communications, classroom techniques, testing and assessment, media and materials, and other reference sources and bibliographies. Entries usually include title, author, availability, and a brief description of the material. Brief sections cover topics such as early childhood, teacher training materials, and places and projects to study and visit. Included is a listing of Massachusetts Title III projects and a selection of ERIC references.

353. Due Process Implementation. A Step by Step Guide: Before, During, After a Fair Hearing. Smyth, Thomas C., Orange County Department of Education, Santa Ana, CA, 1979, 92p (ID 006 011; Reprint: SMERC—HC not available).

This document presents a step by step guide to the processes involved before, during, and after a fair hearing. It is divided into nine parts and contains the following information: Guaranteed Due Process; Parent Procedures to Initiate a Fair Hearing; Choosing a Fair Hearing Panel and Selection of Chairperson; Chairperson's Responsibilities (Before, During, and After), District's Responsibilities (Before, During, and After), and Parent's Responsibilities (Before, During, and After); Sample Forms; Timelines for District Fair Hearing; Timelines for State Review (Hearing); Checklist for Compliance with Public Law 94-142; and Eligibility List for Fair Hearing Panel Members.

354. Guidance Services for the Physically Disabled Two-Year College Student: A Counselor's Manual. State University of New York, Albany, Coordinating Area No. 4, 1978, 167p. Sponsoring agency: New York State Education Department, Albany, Bureau of Two-Year College Programs (ED 161 490; Reprint: EDRS).

This manual, developed to aid in the counseling of handicapped students, is divided according to the various institutional components with which the mainstreamed disabled student deals during the college years. The first section outlines the role of the counseling office in recruiting and preparing for handicapped students, and in serving them during admissions and registration periods, during each semester of attendance, and after graduation. The second section presents challenges to the faculty and discusses the contributions they can make to the successful acclimatization of their handicapped students to college life. In addition to providing information on financial aid resources, the third section discusses the role of the financial aid office during preadmission, admission, and first semester phases of contact. The roles of the health and placement offices during each of these periods are covered in the fourth and fifth sections, while the sixth and seventh sections offer ways of accommodating handicapped patrons in the library and bookstore. The eighth section, dealing with the physical education and recreation needs of the handicapped student, is followed by a section on physically handicapped student representation in student government. The final sections cover self-help organizations and resources, and the role of administrative officials. Extensive resource lists and bibliographies are included.

355. The Handicap Primer: An Introduction to Working with Young Handicapped Children.
Lansdowne, Stephen C., Austin Independent School District, TX, 1978, 66p (ED 155 844; Reprint: EDRS).

The booklet is intended to provide regular class elementary and early childhood teachers with basic information about types of handicaps and teaching strategies to use with exceptional children. An initial section considers the nature of handicaps and the degree of severity of conditions. Reviewed are the following types of exceptionalities: physical disorders (visual impairments, crippling conditions, neurological and other health impairments); communication disorders (auditory impairments, speech disorders, and language disorders); and learning deviations (mental retardation, giftedness, and learning disabilities); behavior disorders; and multiple handicaps. A second section on working with the handicapped considers such practical classroom aspects as to how to act around the handicapped, dealing with medication, and making educational assessment and programing decisions. A final section provides several simulations designed to give the user some idea of what it is like to have a handicap.

356. IEP Handbook: A Teacher Manual for the Implementation of Public Law 94-142. (Project Aid: Assistance for the IEP Development.)
Proger, Barton B. et al., Montgomery County Intermediate Unit 23, Blue Bell, PA, Feb 1978, 189p; some print is marginal and may not reproduce well in hard copy. Sponsoring agency: Bureau of Education for the Handicapped (DHEW/OE), Washington, DC (ED 150 807; Reprint: EDRS).

Designed as a resource guide for teachers, the manual provides information on procedures and forms for developing individualized education programs (IEPs) for handicapped students. An introductory session reviews the purpose of P.L. 94-142 (Education for All Handicapped Children Act) and the law's requirements for IEPs. Presented are sample IEP forms and directions for completing the forms. Among additional IEP-related forms and procedures considered are flow charts for gifted students, forms requesting an IEP planning meeting, referral forms,

notification forms, and due process procedures. A fourth section explains the policies and working procedures of Montgomery County (Pennsylvania) Intermediate Unit regarding IEPs. The bulk of the document consists of appended information, including sample IEPs for students with 15 types of handicapping conditions, and questions and answers on such related areas as IEP content and parental involvement.

357. Individualized Educational Programming: Emphasizing IEPs for Very Young and for Severely Handicapped Learners: (An IEP on IEP).
Pasanella, Anne Langstaff et al., University of Southern California, Los Angeles, School of Education, Aug 1977, 349p; some pages may not reproduce well due to print quality and the use of colored pages in the original document. Sponsoring agency: Bureau of Education for the Handicapped (DHEW/OE), Washington, DC (ED 146 725; Reprint: EDRS).

Presented is a programed manual designed to instruct special educators in the development of individualized educational programs (IEPs) for students with exceptional needs. An introductory section covers the program description, objectives of the program, purpose and rationale, and information on how to use the program. Section II is an overview in which the purpose and structure of the IEP and the team approach to its development are reviewed. Section III focuses on the Total Service Plan, the broad outline of the student's annual program, developed or designed at a meeting of the School Appraisal Team or Educational Assessment Service in which parents are included. Components, covered in individual sections, for the Total Service Plan include present levels of performance, long range goals, annual objectives, placement alternatives, special education services, and evaluation and annual review. Section IV focuses on the Individual Implementation Plan (developed and periodically revised by the teacher in cooperation with specialists and parents) with sections on the following components: short term objectives and learning steps; instructional strategies and techniques; materials and resources; and measurements of student progress. The document contains color-coded sheets—white pages denote general information, green pages denote specific details on very young children, and blue pages denote detailed information related to severely handicapped learners. Appendixes include additional case study examples, a glossary of terms, a posttest, and information on additional resources for each component.

358. Integrating Persons with Handicapping Conditions into Regular Physical Education and Recreation Programs (Revised).
Geddes, Dolores M.; Summerfield, Liane, American Alliance for Health, Physical Education, and Recreation, Washington, DC, Information and Research Utilization Center, Nov 1977, 80p (ED 159 856; Reprint: EDRS—HC not available; also available from American Alliance for Health, Physical Education, and Recreation, 1201 Sixteenth Street, NW, Washington, DC 20036).

The publication contains information pertaining to mainstreaming handicapped students into regular physical education and recreational programs, including an analysis of literature and bibliography. In part 1 terms such as mainstreaming, normalization, impaired, disabled, handicapped, and inconvenienced are clarified, and American Alliance for Health, Physical Education, and Recreation source publications are listed. In part 2, an analysis of literature shows focus on five major areas such as integration of handicapped students into regular school physical educational programs, integration of the handicapped camper into regular camping programs, and the attitudes of participants, peers, and personnel in the integration process. Suggestions are included to aid personnel in the integration process such as the need to stress noncategorical approaches, and the need to provide flexible programs. The bibliography, in part 3, is indexed by handicapping condition, and subject area. Part 4 contains a 261 item, largely annotated bibliography consisting of the following three sections: integration into regular classroom and community situations, integration into regular physical education and recreation programs, and audiovisual materials.

359. Integration and Mainstreaming of Communicatively Disordered Children. Moody, Janet B.; Bozeman, Rhoushelle. Apr 1979, 13p; Paper presented at the Annual International Convention, The Council for Exceptional Children (57th, Dallas, TX, April 22–27, 1979, Session F-2) (ED 171 043; Reprint: EDRS).

The paper presents an overview of the factors involved in providing successful mainstreaming experiences to severely language disordered (SLD) children. Among aspects considered are individualization, behavior management procedures, independent problem solving and decision making, group test taking skills and experiences, social emotional growth, independent living skills, motivation, frustration tolerance, study skills, large group abilities, oral language skills, mathematics abilities, and composition skills. Three areas are emphasized for instruction with SLD children: adaptation of material, directions, and independence. Guidelines are given for allowing student options in materials, sidestepping the students' difficulties with oral directions, and encouraging student independence.

360. An Introduction to Individualized Education Program Plans in Pennsylvania: Guidelines for School Age IEP Development. (Revised January 1978.) Eastern Pennsylvania Regional Resources Center for Special Education, King of Prussia; National Learning Resource Center of Pennsylvania, King of Prussia; Pennsylvania State Department of Education, Harrisburg, Bureau of Special and Compensatory Education. Jan 1978, 143p; some pages may not reproduce clearly due to colored background. Sponsoring agency: Bureau of Education for the Handicapped (DHEW/OE), Washington, DC (EP 165 361; Reprint: EDRS).

The guide, most of which consists of appendixes, forms, and formats, is an introduction to the process of developing individualized education programs (IEPs) for handicapped, gifted, and talented children in the state of Pennsylvania. Instructional components of the IEP are discussed in terms of annual goals, short-term objectives, and determining present educational levels. Some special considerations in IEP plan preparation are reviewed. Procedures for determining educational assignments and developing IEP plans are presented. Among the eight formats and forms provided are a request for permission to evaluate, a due process

notice, and a pre-hearing conference response. Sample IEP plans, a bibliography of instructional objective sources, and guidelines for the preparation of teacher-written objectives are appended.

361. Issues and Answers for Implementing Section 504. National Association of College and University Business Officers, Washington, DC, Jul 1979, 12p (ED 174 167; Reprint: EDRS).

Positions on 37 issues related to higher education's implementation of Section 504 were developed by the National Association of College and University Business Officers (NACUBO). This project is a part of the interassociation effort (Higher Education and the Handicapped—HEATH) to provide colleges and universities with information and technical assistance on Section 504. Section 504 is a civil rights law that guarantees equal opportunities for handicapped persons. The touchstone of Section 504 is integration and not segregation. Separate or different treatment of handicapped persons is only permitted under Section 504 when it is absolutely necessary to achieve full participation. Section 504 mandates the accessibility of programs and activities that already exist, and a full integration of handicapped persons throughout existing programs and institutional structures. The objective of the task force in developing positions on the issues was the achievement of consensus among persons representing diverse backgrounds and interests. The positions represent general consensus of the group, but not all members of the task force are in full agreement with every position.

362. Mainstreaming: 1977 Topical Bibliography. Council for Exceptional Children, Reston, VA, Information Services and Publications, 1977, 24p; Exceptional Child Education Resources Topical Bibliography Series. Sponsoring agency: National Institute of Education (DHEW), Washington, DC (ED 146 739; Reprint: EDRS; also available from The Council for Exceptional Children, ERIC Clearinghouse on Handicapped and Gifted Children, 1920 Association Drive, Reston, VA 22091).

The annotated bibliography includes approximately 95 citations (1973-1976) on mainstreaming exceptional students. It is reported that the information was gathered from volume eight of Exceptional Child Education Resources. Entries are arranged according to accession number and usually include information on author, title, source, date, pagination, availability (including ERIC—Educational Resources Information Center—document number when appropriate), and a brief abstract.

363. Mainstreaming. Special Education Is a Part Of, Not a Part From, Regular Education. Background and Guidelines. Clark, Orville C. 1978, 12p (ED 169 717; Reprint: EDRS).

The document briefly outlines the events leading to mainstreaming of handicapped children and presents guidelines for administrators and teachers involved in implementing mainstream programs. Among suggestions given are the following: the decision to mainstream should be accompanied by a decision to provide a comprehensive instructional support system for the children involved and for their teachers; no mainstreaming effort should be attempted without attention to inservice education; a good working relationship among all staff members involved needs to be established to facilitate mainstreaming; the individual special student under consideration for mainstreaming should be able to successfully compete with his peers in the regular school program for the particular subject, activity, or time period specified; and the mainstreaming process should be a gradual one. Also included is a systematic step-by-step procedure for implementing mainstreaming.

364. **Mainstreaming Exceptional Children: A Guideline for the Principal.** DuClos, Carol et al., Illinois University, Urbana; Lake County Special Education District, Gurnee, IL, Jun 1977, 63p. Sponsoring agency: Illinois State Office of Education, Springfield (ED 151 991; Reprint: EDRS).

Written for the principal, the booklet presents an overview of issues involved in mainstreaming handicapped children. Initial sections address the definition of mainstreaming, the rationale for mainstreaming, and suggestions for supporting the special education teacher. The next three sections concern the administrative and legal aspects of mainstreaming, and present 30 questions and answers about school law. Characteristics and mainstreaming considerations are described for eight types of exceptionalities, including the educationally handicapped and visually impaired. Sample forms are provided of the mainstreaming plan and integration plan.

365. **Mainstreaming Handicapped Students in Vocational Education: A Resource Guide for Vocational Educators.** Brolin, Donn et al., Missouri State Department of Elementary and Secondary Education, Jefferson City; Missouri University, Columbia, Department of Counseling and Personnel Services, Jun 1978, 86p; some pages may not reproduce clearly due to colored background (ED 170 452; Reprint: EDRS).

Designed for vocational educators, seven sections of information concerning vocational education for students with handicaps are provided in this resource guide. Section I provides an overview of major federal legislation, the individualized education program (IEP), and definitions of specific handicaps as defined by Missouri statutes. Section II describes the role and function of a vocational resource educator. Guidelines and considerations for vocational assessment and evaluation are presented in section III. Also included in this section is an annotated bibliography of various assessment instruments (aptitude, interest, and work evaluation). Section IV discusses four areas of concern for accommodating handicapped students: physical environment, curriculum, time requirements, and equipment and materials. Instructional considerations for teaching handicapped students are presented in section V. Topics include the IEP, preparing the classroom environment for mainstreaming, teaching techniques for specific handicapping conditions, classroom organization and management, and community and parent involvement. Section VI discusses job placement, employment, and follow-up. The concluding section contains a list of resource materials (books, guides, bibliographies) and a list of directories of services and materials.

366. **Mainstreaming Preschoolers: Children with Emotional Disturbance. A Guide for Teachers, Parents, and Others Who Work with Emotionally Disturbed Preschoolers.** Lasher, Miriam G. et al., Contract Research Corporation, Belmont, MA, 1978, 154p; parts in colored ink may not reproduce clearly. Sponsoring agency: Administration for Children, Youth, and Families (DHEW), Washington, DC (ED 164 108; Reprint: EDRS; also available from Superintendent of Documents, U.S. Government Printing Office, Washington, DC 20402).

This guide to mainstreaming emotionally disturbed preschoolers is one of a series of eight manuals on mainstreaming preschoolers developed by Project Head Start. The guide is addressed to parents, teachers, and other professionals and paraprofessionals. Chapter I presents information on the meaning, benefits and implementation of mainstreaming and discusses the role of the teacher in mainstreaming. Chapter II discusses local and regional resources and provides information on specialists (psychologists, pediatricians, etc.) who work with emotionally disturbed children. Chapter III focuses on parent/teacher cooperation in developing a program for the handicapped child. Chapter IV discusses the definition of emotional disturbance as well as problems related to the diagnosis and referral of emotionally disturbed children. Chapter V describes the effects of five common categories of emotional disturbance on the preschooler's functioning in the areas of self-concept, social, speech and language, motor, and cognitive development. Chapter VI focuses on planning, arranging classrooms, and teaching mainstreamed emotionally disturbed children. Chapter VII presents information on professional sources of help. Notes on screening and diagnosis are appended.

367. **Mainstreaming Preschoolers: Children with Health Impairments. A Guide for Teachers, Parents, and Others Who Work with Health Impaired Preschoolers.** Healy, Alfred et al., Contract Research Corporation, Belmont, MA, 1978, 139p; parts in colored ink may not reproduce clearly. Sponsoring agency: Administration for Children, Youth, and Families (DHEW), Washington, DC (ED 164 104; Reprint: EDRS; also available from Superintendent of Documents, U.S. Government Printing Office, Washington, DC 20402).

This guide to mainstreaming health impaired preschoolers is one of a series of eight manuals on mainstreaming preschoolers developed by Project Head Start. The guide is addressed to parents, teachers, and other professionals and paraprofessionals. Chapter I presents information on the meaning, benefits, and implementation of mainstreaming. The role of the teacher in mainstreaming is discussed, and sources of assistance are listed. Chapter II distinguishes between handicapping and nonhandicapping health impairments, and defines health impairments as illnesses of a chronic nature or with prolonged convalescence. The following conditions and diseases that result in health impairments are briefly delineated: epilepsy or convulsive disorders, syndromes, pituitary problems, hypothyroidism and diabetes, inborn errors of metabolism, tuberculosis, cystic fibrosis, asthma, congenital heart defects, anemia, hemophilia, and nephrosis, nephritis, and enuresis. Chapter III describes how health impairments affect learning in 3 to 5 year olds, and enumerates measures to take in emergency situations. Chapter IV focuses on planning, arranging classrooms, and teaching mainstreamed health impaired children. Chapter V describes how parents and teachers can work together while chapters VI and VII provide information on possible resources and sources of help, professional and otherwise. Notes on screening and diagnosis are appended.

368. Mainstreaming Preschoolers: Children with Hearing Impairment. A Guide for Teachers, Parents, and Others Who Work with Hearing Impaired Preschoolers. LaPorta, Rita Ann et al., Contract Research Corporation, Belmont, MA, 1978, 138p; parts in colored ink may not reproduce clearly. Sponsoring agency: Administration for Children, Youth, and Families (DHEW), Washington, DC (ED 164 109; Reprint EDRS; also available from Superintendent of Documents, U.S. Government Printing Office, Washington, DC 20402).

This guide to mainstreaming preschoolers with hearing impairments is one of a series of eight manuals on mainstreaming preschoolers developed by Project Head Start. The guide is addressed to parents, teachers, and other professionals and paraprofessionals. Chapter I presents information on the meaning, benefits, and implementation of mainstreaming. The role of the teacher in mainstreaming is discussed, and sources of assistance are listed. Chapter II provides the Head Start definition (and other common definitions) of hearing loss and discusses categories of hearing impairment, types and causes of hearing loss, and problems in diagnosis and referral. Chapter III describes the development and functioning of children with all levels of hearing impairments in four basic areas: communication skills, social and emotional development, cognitive skills, and motor skills. Chapter IV presents information on planning, arranging classrooms, and teaching mainstreamed hearing impaired children. Chapter V focuses on parent/teacher cooperation while Chapters VI and VII provide information on specialists, organizations, and publications that can provide help. Notes on screening and diagnosis are appended.

369. Mainstreaming Preschoolers: Children with Learning Disabilities. A Guide for Teachers, Parents, and Others Who Work with Learning Disabled Preschoolers. Hayden, Alice H. et al., Contract Research Corporation, Belmont, MA, 1978, 140p; parts in colored ink may not reproduce clearly. Sponsoring agency: Administration for Children, Youth, and Families (DHEW), Washington, DC (ED 164 110; Reprint: EDRS; also available from Superintendent of Documents, U.S. Government Printing Office, Washington, DC 20402).

This guide to mainstreaming preschoolers with learning disabilities is one of a series of eight manuals on mainstreaming preschoolers developed by Project Head Start. The guide is addressed to parents, teachers, and other professionals and paraprofessionals. Chapter I presents information on the meaning, benefits, and implementation of mainstreaming. The role of the teacher in mainstreaming is discussed, and sources of assistance with a handicapped child are listed. Chapter II looks at definitions of learning disabilities and describes the behavioral characteristics of various learning disabilities. An observation checklist and general guidelines for recognizing problems for referral are included. Chapter III briefly describes development in learning disabled and nonhandicapped children and discusses some of the observable behaviors exhibited by learning disabled children in six skill areas: motor, visual, auditory, communicative, cognitive, and social skills. Chapter IV focuses on planning, arranging classrooms, and teaching mainstreamed learning disabled children. Chapter V describes how parents and teachers can work together while Chapters VI and VII provide information on professional sources of help. Notes on screening and diagnosis are appended.

370. Mainstreaming Preschoolers: Children with Mental Retardation. A Guide for Teachers, Parents, and Others Who Work with Mentally Retarded Preschoolers. Lynch, Eleanor Whiteside et al., Contract Research Corporation, Belmont, MA, 1978, 146p; parts in colored ink may not reproduce clearly. Sponsoring agency: Administration for Children, Youth, and Families (DHEW), Washington, DC (ED 164 103; Reprint: EDRS; also available from Superintendent of Documents, U.S. Government Printing Office, Washington, DC 20402).

This guide to mainstreaming mentally retarded preschoolers is one of a series of eight manuals on mainstreaming preschoolers developed by Project Head Start. The guide is addressed to parents, teachers, and other professionals and paraprofessionals. Chapter I presents information on the meaning, benefits, and implementation of mainstreaming and discusses the role of the teacher. Chapter II defines mental retardation, focusing on levels of retardation, rate of learning, commonly associated handicaps, and diagnostic problems. An observational checklist and general guidelines for identifying children for referral are included. Chapter III discusses how mental retardation affects learning and development in three to five year olds and describes children with mild, moderate, and severe handicaps. Chapter IV focuses on planning, physical setting, and teaching techniques for mainstreamed mentally retarded children. Chapter V discusses parent/teacher cooperation, while Chapters VI and VII provide information on specialists, organizations, and other sources of help. Notes on screening and diagnosis are appended.

371. Mainstreaming Preschoolers: Children with Orthopedic Handicaps. A Guide for Teachers, Parents, and Others Who Work with Orthopedically Handicapped Preschoolers. Kieran, Shari Stokes et al., Contract Research Corporation, Belmont, MA, 1978, 146p; parts in colored ink may not reproduce clearly. Sponsoring agency: Administration for Children, Youth, and Families (DHEW), Washington, DC (ED 164 107; Reprint: EDRS; also available from Superintendent of Documents, U.S. Government Printing Office, Washington, DC 20402).

This guide to mainstreaming preschoolers with orthopedic handicaps is one of a series of eight manuals on mainstreaming preschoolers developed by Project Head Start. The guide is addressed to parents, teachers, and other professionals and paraprofessionals. Chapter I presents information on the meaning, benefits, and implementation of mainstreaming. The role of the teacher in mainstreaming is discussed, and sources of assistance are listed. Chapter II discusses local and regional resources and provides specialists (occupational therapists, orthopedists, physical therapists, etc.) who work with handicapped children. Chapter III focuses on parent/teacher cooperation. Chapter IV discusses various kinds of orthopedic handicaps (such as cerebal palsy, spinal cord damage, arthritis, muscular dystrophy) and associated problems, and ways of recognizing problems for referral. Chapter V discusses how orthopedic handicaps can affect a child's functioning and learning. Chapter VI focuses on planning, arranging classrooms, and teaching mainstreamed orthopedically handicapped children. Chapter VII presents information on professionals, organizations, and other sources of help. Notes on screening and diagnosis are appended.

372. Mainstreaming Preschoolers: Children with Speech and Language Impairments. A Guide for Teachers, Parents, and Others Who Work with Speech and Language Impaired Preschoolers.
Liebergott, Jacqueline et al., Contract Research Corporation, Belmont, MA, 1978, 174p; parts in colored ink may not reproduce clearly. Sponsoring agency: Administration for Children, Youth, and Families (DHEW), Washington, DC (ED 164 106; Reprint: EDRS; also available from Superintendent of Documents, U.S. Government Printing Office, Washington, DC 20402).

This guide to mainstreaming preschoolers with speech and language impairments is one of a series of eight manuals on mainstreaming preschoolers developed by Project Head Start. The guide is addressed to parents, teachers, and other professionals and paraprofessionals. Chapter I presents information on the meaning, benefits, and implementation of mainstreaming. The role of the teacher in mainstreaming is discussed, and possible resources s/he can tap for asistance with a handicapped child are listed. Chapter II describes various speech and language impairments (stuttering, chronic voice disorders, and articulation problems), commonly associated handicaps, and ways to identify them in young children. Information on distinguishing between true speech and language impairments and simple differences in children's speech for referral purposes is included. Chapter III contains detailed information on the normal development of communication skills and explains how various communication disorders can affect the cognitive, social, motor, and communicative functioning, and the development of self-concept in 3 to 5 year olds. Chapter IV focuses on planning, arranging classrooms, and teaching mainstreamed children with speech/language impairments. Chapters V through VII describe parent/teacher cooperation and professional sources of help. Notes on diagnosis and screening are appended.

373. Mainstreaming Preschoolers: Children with Visual Handicaps. A Guide for Teachers, Parents, and Others Who Work with Visually Handicapped Preschoolers.
Alonso, Lou et al., Contract Research Corporation, Belmont, MA, 1978, 134p; parts in colored ink may not reproduce clearly. Sponsoring agency: Administration for Children, Youth, and Families (DHEW), Washington, DC (ED 164 105; Reprint: EDRS; also available from Superintendent of Documents, U.S. Government Printing Office, Washington, DC 20402).

This guide to mainstreaming visually handicapped preschoolers is one of a series of eight manuals on mainstreaming preschoolers developed by Project Head Start. The guide is addressed to parents, teachers, and other professionals and paraprofessionals. Chapter I presents information on the meaning, benefits, and implementation of mainstreaming. The role of the teacher in mainstreaming is discussed, and possible resources she can tap for assistance with a handicapped child are listed. Chapter II provides a definition of visual handicaps and discusses problems in diagnosis and referral of visually handicapped preschoolers. An observational checklist for diagnosis and general guidelines on referral are included. Chapter III discusses how visually handicapped children function in various areas of development; self-concept, motor skills, self-help skills, cognitive skills, language and speech skills, and social skills. Chapter IV focuses on specific aspects of mainstreaming visually handicapped children such as planning, physical setting, and classroom facilities, general teaching guidelines, and specific teaching techniques and learning activities. Chapter V describes how parents and teachers can work together as partners, while chapters VI and VII provide information on possible resources and sources of help, professional and otherwise. Notes on screening and diagnosis are appended.

374. Mainstreaming the Physically Handicapped Student for Team Sports.
Grosse, Susan J., American Alliance for Health, Physical Education, and Recreation, Washington, DC, Jan 1978, 9p (ED 165 350; Reprint EDRS—HC not available; also available from American Alliance for Health, Physical Education and Recreation, 1201 16th Street, NW, Washington, DC 20036).

The article gives suggestions for mainstreaming physically handicapped students into regular physical education classes during instruction team sports. The report lists six pointers for general class organization and instruction, such as establishing an atmosphere of acceptance, emphasizing the positive contributions each student can make, and requiring all students' participation in pre-play activities. Suggestions for stationary practice and moving drills are given, as are hints for facilitating the handicapped individual's participation in game play. Specific suggestions for the participation of the handicapped are listed for the following sports: basketball, floor hockey, football, soccer, and softball.

375. Mainstreaming the Visually Impaired Child.
Calovini, Gloria, Illinois State Office of Education, Springfield, 43p; two report forms on pages 36 and 37 may be marginally legible due to small print of original document. Sponsoring agency: Bureau of Education for the Handicapped (DHEW/OE), Washington, DC (ED 140 540; Reprint: EDRS).

Intended for school administrators and regular classroom teachers, the document presents guidelines for working with visually impaired students being integrated into regular classes. Included is a description of the special education program in Illinois. Sections cover the following topics: identification and referral of visually impaired students; characteristics of the visually impaired; guidelines for the teacher, such as classroom arrangement and management; educational materials and equipment; social behavior and mannerisms; daily living skills; and the contributions of school personnel serving the visually impaired. Appended are a listing of additional references and the addresses of private and public agencies in Illinois serving the visually handicapped.

376. Mark and Amy: The Disturbing Children in Your Classroom. Gear, Gayle et al., Alabama University, Birmingham, School of Education, 1979, 33p. Sponsoring agency: Bureau of Education for the Handicapped (DHEW/OE), Washington, DC, Division of Personnel Preparation (ED 176 455; Reprint EDRS—HC not available; also available from The Interrelated Teacher Education Project, The University of Alabama, Birmingham, AL 35294).

Intended for regular class teachers, the booklet provides information to aid in mainstreaming the emotionally disturbed (ED) child. Sections address the following areas: characteristics of the ED child (identification, theories on behavioral problems, the Pupil Behavior Rating Scale); teaching methods (general guidelines and guidelines for dealing with the withdrawn child who is inattentive, the withdrawn child who is overly dependent, and the acting out child); and resources on ED children.

377. Matt: The Mentally Retarded Child in Your Classroom. Gear, Gayle et al., Alabama University, Birmingham, School of Education, 1979, 36p. Sponsoring agency: Bureau of Education for the Handicapped (DHEW/OE), Washington, DC, Division of Personnel Preparation (ED 176 457; Reprint: EDRS—HC not available; also available from The Interrelated Teacher Education Project, The University of Alabama, Birmingham, AL 35294).

Intended for regular class teachers, the booklet provides information to aid in mainstreaming the mentally retarded (MR) child. Sections address the following areas: reasons for mainstreaming the MR student; definition of mental retardation; assessment (areas of assessment and suggested evaluation measures, the assessment team); suggested readings for teachers and students on the retarded; personalized curricula (suggestions for instruction relating to intellectual functioning, abstract thinking, language development, physical maturation, short term memory, attention span, and self concept); and general teaching techniques for the MR child.

378. Needs Assessment Procedure: Mainstreaming Handicapped. Volume II. A Manual for Vocational Education Administrators. Final Report. Hughes, James H.; Rice, Eric, System Sciences, Inc., Chapel Hill, NC, May 1978, 88p. Sponsoring agency: Bureau of Occupational and Adult Education (DHEW/OE), Washington, DC, Division of Research and Demonstration (ED 160 892; Reprint: EDRS).

Intended to assist local vocational education administrators in needs assessment and planning procedures for mainstreaming handicapped students, this manual presents a five-step process: (1) needs assessment and barrier identification (includes instruction in the nominal group technique process); (2) goal, objective, and strategy development (a general planning model is presented along with instructions on formation of a local planning committee); (3) criteria and process for strategy selection (use of the Force Field Analysis technique is presented); (4) planning activities for strategy implementation; and (5) planning for evaluation (types of evaluation, measurements, and preparation of an evaluation plan are discussed). Included in the appendixes are an instructional pamphlet

which gives an overview of mainstreaming (history, legislation, definition) and lists of resources: organizations, institutions, and agencies; instructional materials (names, addresses, and brief description given); and planning materials (names, addresses, and brief description given).

379. Pilot Models for Mainstreaming Secondary Students Who Are Mild to Moderate Behaviorally Disordered: Administrator Manual. Toker, Mary Lou et al., Nebraska State Department of Education, Lincoln, Jun 1976, 111p; ESEA Title IV-C Validated Project: Recognize, Respond, Reinforce; some pages have poor print and may not reproduce well in hard copy. Sponsoring agency: Bureau of Elementary and Secondary Education (DHEW/OE), Washington, DC (ED 155 854; Reprint: EDRS).

The administrator manual describes a program model for delivery of services, within the concept of mainstreaming, to secondary students who are mild to moderate behaviorally disordered. Four sections cover the following project components (subsection topics are in parentheses): introductory information (goal, philosophy, and use of the guide); project overview (statement of need, history, and evaluation); program selection-management considerations (project components and resources); and local application of the program (needs identification; design, implementation, and monitoring; and evaluation). The bulk of the document consists of a glossary and appendixes on the definition of mainstreaming, a project overview, and project resources.

380. Pilot Models for Mainstreaming Secondary Students Who Are Mild to Moderate Behaviorally Disordered: Resource Teacher Manual. Toker, Mary Lou et al., Nebraska State Department of Education, Lincoln, 1978, 244p; ESEA Title IV-C Validated Project: Recognize, Respond, Reinforce; some pages have poor print and will not reproduce well in hard copy. Sponsoring agency: Bureau of Elementary and Secondary Education (DHEW/OE), Washington, DC (ED 155 853; Reprint: EDRS).

The resource teacher manual describes a program model for delivery of services, within the concept of mainstreaming, to secondary students who are mild to moderate behaviorally disordered. Following introductory and overview sections, a student placement section discusses student screening, diagnosis, and placement procedures and gives examples and information on four screening instruments: the Project Screening Instrument, the Attitude toward School Scale, the Self-Concept as a Learner Scale, and the Student Screening-Monitoring Profile Form. A fourth section focuses on teaching strategies and techniques. The bulk of this section consists of a listing of reference materials, as well as charts on student materials which are subdivided in the following areas: interest and motivation, art, English, mathematics, reading, spelling, values guidance, and vocational education. Section V on supplementary services examines ongoing observation-assessment techniques, a monitoring model, and parent involvement procedures. A final section reviews exit and follow-through procedures. Also included are a glossary and appendixes on a descriptive definition of mainstreaming, a project overview, and student examples.

381. Project HAPI: Handicapped Achievement Program Improvement (Assessment Handbooks: Hearing Impaired). San Diego County Superintendent of Schools Office, CA, Oct 1977, 71p (ID 005 839; Reprint: SMERC—HC not available).

This HAPI Project assessment manual was designed as a resource guide for practical assessment of students who are hearing impaired. Assessment tools are described in terms of format, time, age, grade level, normative data, and source. Assessment materials not readily available from standard sources are included, along with sample forms used in organizing the assessment information.

382. Project HAPI: Handicapped Achievement Program Improvement (Assessment Handbooks; Language, Speech, Hearing, Severe Language Handicap). San Diego County Superintendent of Schools Office, CA, Oct 1977, 79p (ID 005 838; Reprint: SMERC—HC not available).

This HAPI Project assessment manual was designed as a resource guide for practical assessment of students with language, speech, hearing, and severe language handicaps. Assessment tools are described in terms of format, time, age, grade level, normative data, and source. Assessment materials not readily available from standard sources are included, along with sample forms used in organizing the assessment information.

383. Project HAPI: Handicapped Achievement Program Improvement (Assessment Handbooks: Learning Handicapped). San Diego County Superintendent of Schools Office, CA, Oct 1977, 95p (ID 005 841; Reprint: SMERC—HC not available).

This HAPI Project assessment manual was designed as a resource guide for practical assessment of students who are learning handicapped. Assessment tools are described in terms of format, time, age, grade level, normative data, and source. Assessment materials not readily available from standard sources are included, along with sample forms used in organizing the assessment information.

384. Project HAPI: Handicapped Achievement Program Improvement (Assessment Handbooks: Trainable Mentally Retarded; Developmentally Handicapped). San Diego County Superintendent of Schools Office, CA, Oct 1977, 100p (ID 005 840; Reprint: SMERC—HC not available).

This HAPI Project assessment manual was designed as a resource guide for practical assessment of students who are trainable mentally retarded or developmentally handicapped. Assessment tools are described in terms of format, time, age, grade level, normative data, and source. Assessment materials not readily available from standard sources are included, along with sample forms used in organizing the assessment information.

385. Project HAPI: Handicapped Achievement Program Improvement (Assessment Handbooks: Visually Impaired). San Diego County Superintendent of Schools Office, CA, Oct 1977, 134p (ID 005 842; Reprint: SMERC—HC not available).

This HAPI Project assessment manual was designed as a resource guide for practical assessment of students who are visually impaired. Assessment tools are described in terms of format, time, age, grade level, normative data, and source. Assessment materials not readily available from standard sources are included, along with sample forms used in organizing the assessment information.

386. Project HAPI: Handicapped Achievement Program Improvement (Intervention Handbook: Hearing Impaired). San Diego County Superintendent of Schools Office, CA, Oct 1977, 67p (ID 005 845; Reprint: SMERC—HC not available).

A key component of an individualized education program (IEP), as mandated by Public Law 94-142, is the intervention methods and materials section. The purpose of this handbook is to provide a compilation of intervention resources that can be used for individualized education planning, and sample IEP forms. In addition to the resource matrix for published materials, samples of those unpublished, an education plan checklist, a P.L. 94-142 requirements checklist, and sample IEP forms are included. Materials in this handbook are for hearing impaired students.

387. Project HAPI: Handicapped Achievement Program Improvement (Intervention Handbook: Language, Speech, Hearing, Severe Language Handicapped). San Diego County Superintendent of Schools Office, CA, Oct 1977, 83p (ID 005 844; Reprint: SMERC—HC not available).

A key component of an individualized education program (IEP), as mandated by Public Law 94-142, is the intervention methods and materials section. The purpose of this handbook is to provide a compilation of intervention resources that can be used for individualized education planning, and sample IEP forms. In addition to the resource matrix for published materials, samples of those unpublished, an education plan checklist, a P.L. 94-142 requirements checklist, and sample IEP forms are included. Materials in this handbook are for language, speech, hearing, and severe language handicapped students.

388. Project HAPI: Handicapped Achievement Program Improvement (Intervention Handbook: Learning Handicapped). San Diego County Superintendent of Schools Office, CA, Oct 1977, 104p (ID 005 847; Reprint: SMERC—HC not available).

A key component of an individualized education program (IEP), as mandated by Public Law 94-142, is the intervention methods and materials section. The purpose of this handbook is to provide a compilation of intervention resources that can be used for individualized education planning, and sample IEP forms. In addition to the resource matrix for published materials, samples of those unpublished, an education plan checklist, a P.L. 94-142 requirements checklist, and sample IEP forms are included. Materials in this handbook are for learning handicapped students.

389. Project HAPI: Handicapped Achievement Program Improvement (Intervention Handbook: Trainable Mentally Retarded; Developmentally Handicapped). San Diego County Superintendent of Schools Office, CA, Oct 1977, 160p (ID 005 846; Reprint: SMERC—HC not available).

A key component of an individualized education program (IEP), as mandated by Public Law 94-142, is the intervention methods and materials section. The purpose of this handbook is to provide a compilation of intervention resources that can be used for individualized education planning, and sample IEP forms. In addition to the resource matrix for published materials, samples of those unpublished, an education plan checklist, a P.L. 94-142 requirements checklist, and sample IEP forms are included. Materials in this handbook are for trainable mentally retarded or developmentally handicapped students.

390. Project HAPI: Handicapped Achievement Program Improvement (Intervention Handbook: Visually Impaired). San Diego County Superintendent of Schools Office, CA, Oct 1977, 100p (ID 005 848; Reprint: SMERC—HC not available).

A key component of an individualized education program (IEP), as mandated by Public Law 94-142, is the intervention methods and materials section. The purpose of this handbook is to provide a compilation of intervention resources that can be used for individualized education planning, and sample IEP forms. In addition to the resource matrix for published materials, samples of those unpublished, an education plan checklist, a P.L. 94-142 requirements checklist, and sample IEP forms are included. Materials in this handbook are for visually impaired students.

391. Project Team: Teacher Encouragement to Activate Mainstreaming: Administrative and Resource Personnel Kit. Fullerton Union High School District, CA, Aug 1977, 50p; parts may reproduce poorly due to ink and paper colors (ED 149 494; Reprint: EDRS).

Presented is the administrative and resource personnel kit developed as part of Project TEAM (Teacher Encouragement to Activate Mainstreaming) to improve attitudes and skills of regular secondary teachers working with educable mentally retarded or educationally handicapped students. Sections of the kit include an introduction, a listing of the study's significant findings and conclusions (such as enthusiasm for mainstreaming by teacher and student participants), forms and guidelines for mainstreaming preparation, suggested agendas for staff development programs, forms for use in the resource program, and a list of selected references.

392. Project Team: Teacher Encouragement to Activate Mainstreaming: Teacher Handbook. Fullerton Union High School District, CA, Aug 1977, 50p; parts may reproduce poorly due to ink and paper colors (ED 149 495; Reprint: EDRS).

Presented is the teacher handbook developed as part of Project TEAM (Teacher Encouragement to Activate Mainstreaming) to improve attitudes and skills of regular secondary teachers working with educable mentally handicapped or educationally handicapped students. Sections of the handbook include an introduction, a brief consideration of classroom management, a flowchart for the selection of course objectives, guidelines for personalizing instruction, hints for problem solving, a suggestions chart offering specific strategies to change behaviors exhibited in the classroom, a case study, and a glossary of about 50 terms such as aphasia and directionality.

393. Randy: The Learning Disabled Child in Your Classroom. Gear, Gayle et al., Alabama University, Birmingham, School of Education, 1979, 28p. Sponsoring agency: Bureau of Education for the Handicapped (DHEW/OE), Washington, DC, Division of Personnel Preparation (ED 176 454; Reprint EDRS—HC not available; also available from The Interrelated Teacher Education Project, The University of Alabama, Birmingham, AL 35294).

Intended for regular class teachers, the booklet provides information to aid in mainstreaming the learning disabled (LD) child. Sections address the following areas: characteristics of the LD child (legal definition, areas of difficulty); educational assessment (the assessment team, types of tests); reading; mathematics (specific arithmetic programs); effective teaching methods, and resources on learning disabilities.

394. A Reference System to Published IEP Resources for Educational Assessment and Programming. Dutt, Susan; Forte, Sheryl, Lancaster-Lebanon Intermediate Unit 13, Lancaster, PA, 1978, 178p (ED 159 846; Reprint: EDRS).

The document provides a reference system to published materials which have been found useful in the development of individualized education plans as prescribed by P.L. 94-142, the Education for All Handicapped Children Act. The system is designed to provide ordering information and a description of resource materials, which include tests, curriculum guides, and sequenced objectives. Following an introductory section with information on using the system are sections consisting of an alphabetical listing of materials, an index of materials, descriptions of materials, and a publishers key.

395. Sourcebook: Science Education and the Physically Handicapped. Hofman, Helenmarie H.; Ricker, Kenneth S., National Science Teachers Association, Washington, DC, 1979, 278p; not available in hard copy due to copyright restrictions (ED 176 980; Reprint: EDRS—HC not available; also available from National Science Teachers Association, 1742 Connecticut Ave, NW, Washington, DC 20009).

Addressed is the increased need for information on science education and the physically handicapped following enactment of the Education of the Handicapped Act. The document is divided into ten sections including: (1) Science Education and the Handicapped; (2) Science for Everyone (mainstreaming); (3) Preparing Teachers to Work with the Handicapped; (4) Resources for Teachers/Schools; (5) Science and the Auditory Handicapped; (6) Science and the Orthopedic Handicapped; (7) Science and the Visually Handicapped; (8) Extending the Science Program Beyond the School; (9) Handicapped and Careers in Science; and (10) Implications for the Future.

396. Staff Instructions for Implementing Title V Regulations/Public Law 94-142 Regulations Including Parents/Guardians Rights and Responsibilities (Includes Text in Spanish). Santa Clara County Superintendent of Schools Office, CA, Sep 1977, 72p (ID 005 683; Reprint: SMERC—HC not available).

This document is a collection of forms, regulations, materials, suggestions, background readings, and guidelines, for staff members charged with compliance and implementation of P.L. 94-142, the Education for All Handicapped Children Act. The majority of the forms deal with keeping parents informed of their rights and responsibilities under this Act. With the exception of the glossary and the "Parent/Guardian and School Staff Planning Conference for the Individual Education Plan," all materials are in both English and Spanish.

397. Supportive Services for Special Needs Students in Mainstreamed Vocational Education Programs: Guidelines for Implementation. National Evaluation Systems, Inc., Amherst, MA, Apr 1979, 73p. Sponsoring agency: West Virginia State Department of Education, Charleston, WV; Bureau of Vocational, Technical, and Adult Education (ED 174 836; Reprint: EDRS).

Designed for vocational instructors and local school administrative personnel, these guidelines suggest ways for improving the vocational education of mainstreamed special needs students by providing supportive services to best meet the needs of the visually handicapped, orthopedically impaired, seriously emotionally disturbed, or learning disabled. The first of six sections discusses the identification of and prescription for students with special needs. Section 2 relates instructional supportive services and the role of the vocational instructor. The third section expands upon the relationship of guidance and counseling services and the role of the vocational instructor. Section 4 discusses the identification of job opportunities, job placement, and follow-up services and the role of the vocational instructor. The fifth section describes corrective and other supportive services designed specifically for those students with physical related problems and supportive services available outside the local school. The final section describes funding provisions for excess costs involved in providing supportive services for special needs students in regular vocational education programs. A sample listing of out-of-school support agencies providing support to persons with disabilities is given.

398. Teaching the Special Child in Regular Classrooms. Klein, Jenni, ERIC Clearinghouse on Early Childhood Education, Urbana, IL; Office of Child Development (DHEW), Washington, DC, 1977, 77p. Sponsoring agency: National Institute of Education (DHEW), Washington, DC (ED 136 902; Reprint: EDRS; also available from ERIC Clearinghouse on Early Childhood Education, University of Illinois, 805 West Pennsylvania Avenue, Urbana, IL 61801).

This document includes a paper and a bibliography of ERIC abstracts on teaching the special child in mainstreamed classrooms. The paper presents five basic assumptions related to the teaching of young handicapped children, discusses principles of teaching special children which may be helpful to teachers working in mainstreamed classrooms, and looks briefly at the unresolved questions associated with teaching special children. The principles of teaching young handicapped children are based on the assumptions that: (1) the handicapped child has the same basic needs as all children; (2) handicapping conditions involve the whole child, not just the affected organ, limb, or function; (3) handicapped children are individuals; (4) a handicap cannot be overlooked; and (5) handicapped children are entitled to equal opportunities to learn and develop. Teaching young handicapped children requires special knowledge and understanding, active intervention on behalf of the child, and orchestration of the many facets of a total program. The problems of mainstreaming, labeling, age of enrollment, and readiness are discussed. The selected ERIC bibliography on mainstreaming handicapped children includes resumes from "Resources in Education" (RIE), October 1976 through January 1977, and citations from "Current Index to Journals in Education" (CIJE), September 1976 through January 1977.

399. Tips on Mainstreaming: Do's and Don'ts in Activity Programs. American Alliance for Health, Physical Education, and Recreation, Washington, DC, Information and Research Utilization Center, Mar 1978, 17p (ED 165 437; Reprint: EDRS—HC not available; also available from American Alliance for Health, Physical Education, and Recreation, 1201 Sixteenth Street, NW, Washington, DC 20036).

The document provides 10 brief articles on activities for mainstreamed handicapped students. Included are the following titles: "Tips on Mainstreaming—Do's and Don'ts for Activity Programs"; "Mainstreaming—A Goal and A Process"; "What to Do When You Meet a Handicapped Person"; "Tips for Dealing with Handicapped Persons"; "Relating to Orthopedically and Visually Handicapped Individuals"; "Making Relationships More Comfortable between Blind and Sighted Individuals"; "When You Have a Hearing Impaired Player on the Team or in Class"; "Communicating with Hearing Impaired Persons in One- to-One and Group Situations"; "First Steps in Mainstreaming"; and "Mainstreaming Does Work."

400. Vocational Education for the Handicapped: A Review. Information Series No. 119. Hull, Marc E., Ohio State University, Columbus, ERIC Clearinghouse on Career Education, 1977, 67p. Sponsoring agency: National Institute of Education (DHEW), Washington, DC (ED 149 188; Reprint: EDRS; also available from National Center for Research in Vocational Education Publications, Ohio State University, 1960 Kenny Road, Columbus, OH 43210).

A review and synthesis of programming and techniques useful in providing vocational education to handicapped secondary and postsecondary school students is presented in this information analysis paper. Information and insights are given so that vocational administrators and supervisors can assess their efforts to provide equal opportunities for the handicapped to participate fully in all facets of vocational education including youth organizations, cooperative vocational education, vocational guidance services, and consumer education. Also, practical suggestions are included for effectively accommodating handicapped students through both regular and special instructional arrangements. Specific topics discussed include the following: rationale for the participation of the handicapped in vocational education, barriers to participation, impact of legislation, identifying the handicapped, developing appropriate program alternatives for serving the handicapped, prevocational education, role of vocational education in comprehensive secondary programing for the academically handicapped, need for interagency cooperation, curriculum and instructional materials to assist in vocational training, personnel preparation, evaluation of students and programs, and professional organizations. The conclusion is made that emphasis of the future must be one of equal access and maximum accommodation. The appendix contains descriptions of information systems on the handicapped.

BOOKS

401. Administration of Mainstreaming: The Best of ERIC No. 49. ERIC Clearinghouse on Education Management. Eugene, OR: University of Oregon, 1980, 4p.

Cites 12 ERIC microfiche and journal articles.

402. Classroom Strategies to Aid the Disabled Learner: with Glossary. † Abbott, Jean. Cambridge, MA: Educators Publishing Service, 1978, 71p.

Intended for secondary and middle school teachers of mainstreamed learning disabled (LD) students, the book discusses classroom strategies and suggestions. After an introductory chapter on educational and psychological characteristics of LD students, the text proceeds to touch upon etiology, learning characteristics (examples of visual, auditory, and processing distortions), and learning styles. Classroom strategies are examined for the visual learner, auditory learner, distractible learner, and disorganized learner. Two final chapters address implications of Public Law 94-142, the Education for All Handicapped Children Act.

403. The Communicatively Disordered Child: Management Procedures for the Classroom. McCartan, Kathleen W. Austin, TX: Learning Concepts, 1977, 102p.

This book was written to assist the classroom teacher in carrying out teacher responsibilities in working with communicatively disordered children. Utilizing a cartoon format, it provides definitions, theories about causes, characteristics, guidelines for referral, and practical classroom activities relating to articulation disorders, voice disorders, stuttering, and communication and language disorders.

404. Community Competencies for the Handicapped. School Graduation Requirements: A Basis for Curriculum and IEP Development. † Stewart, Jim et al. Springfield, IL: Charles C Thomas, 1978, 198p.

The book defines skills and presents an individualized learning program for teaching independent community living skills to handicapped students. Provided are four levels of competencies which range from "dependent" to "independent" functioning, a framework for a curriculur scope and sequence, a basis from which teachers can generate appropriate goals and short term objectives, and a graduation system compatible with the graduation systems for nonhandicapped students. It is explained that the competencies are divided into the following ten areas of study: language arts/English, mathematics, social studies/history, citizenship/government, science, health education, physical education, consumer education/economics/personal finance, career education, and elective/selective. It is explained that each competency has at least one performance indicator which is a measurable statement by which the student will be judged to have attained the competency. Outlined are the procedures for using the book to generate the long term or annual goals and measurable short term objectives required by Public Law 94-142 (the Education for All Handicapped Children Act).

405. Curriculum Analysis and Design for Retarded Learners. † Klein, Nancy Krow et al. Columbus, OH: Charles E. Merrill Publishing Co., 1979, 372p.

The book presents a systems analysis approach to curriculum analysis and design for mainstreamed mentally handicapped students. Mental retardation is defined, and its etiology is explored along with personality development and learning characteristics of retarded students. Pupil assessment is discussed in terms of such aspects as identification and placement, adaptive behavior, the teacher's role, and individualized education programs. Educational settings for retarded students are examined from the standpoint of E. Deno's cascade system of instructional alternatives. Educational goals for the retarded learner are reviewed in terms of the needs and skills of individual learners, the needs of contemporary society, and the knowledge and skills inherent in subject matter mastery; and a Functional life approach to curriculum design is presented. The analysis of curriculum content is discussed, including content analysis and criterion testing, and illustrative examples are provided. Several principles for selecting and implementing learning activities are presented, including active learning, variety, practice, feedback, and reinforcement. Classroom evaluation is discussed in terms of such things as measurement, testing, and validity. Also covered are the writing of useful objectives and the analysis of curriculum materials.

406. Education of the Severely/Profoundly Handicapped: What is the Least Restrictive Alternative? Gentry, N. Dale; Parks, A. Lee. Austin, TX: Learning Concepts, 1977, 116p.

Utilizing a cartoon format, this book provides classroom teachers with the following types of information on the severely/profoundly handicapped: education (historical perspective, definitions, trends in service, least restrictive setting); assessment and curriculum (medical and educational assessment, curriculum areas, and programs); and teaching strategies (behavioral principles, data collection, task analysis, and case studies).

407. Exceptional Children: Introduction to Special Education. † Hallahan, Daniel P.; Kaufmann, James M. Englewood Cliffs, NJ: Prentice-Hall, 1978, 497p.

Intended for both regular and special education teachers as well as parents of handicapped children, this book presents a general introduction to the characteristics of exceptional children and the various ways in which they are educated. Although the major emphasis is placed on the techniques and classroom practices that make up the discipline of special education, the special psychological, medical, and sociological aspects of each handicapping condition are also described. Chapter 1 presents an introduction to the historical concepts surrounding exceptional children and the major trends and issues pertaining to the field. Each of the remaining eight chapters is devoted to one of the traditional categorical areas of special education: Chapter 2, Mental Retardation; Chapter 3, Learning Disabilities; Chapter 4, Emotional Disturbance; Chapter 5, Speech and Language Disorders; Chapter 6, Hearing Impairment; Chapter 7, Visual Impairment; Chapter 8, Physical Handicaps; and Chapter 9, Giftedness. Included at the end of each chapter are a summary, references, and a section entitled "Managing the Child in School" which presents general principles for regular and special education teachers to follow. A Glossary of special education terms is also included.

408. Getting It Together with P.L. 94-142: A Practical Guide to IEP Development and Implementation.† Hedbring, Charles. Greenwich, NY: Hedbring Associates, Program Steppe, 1977, 147p.

The manual discusses step by step development of IEPs (individualized education programs) for handicapped children, as mandated in Public Law 94-142, the Education for All Handicapped Children Act. The first section reviews the background and scope of P.L. 94-142, while the second focuses on ten steps in the development of IEPs, including selecting an assessment guide, listing instructional objectives, developing logical task analyses, graphing, and promoting generalization. The next section considers steps in building a curriculum file (such as selecting and listing instructional objectives, determining prerequisites, and developing logical task analyses for each of the objectives and prerequisites). Five steps in building a student file are explained to include separating behavioral objectives into short term objectives and annual goals and graphing student performance. A final section contains an IEP program analysis checklist covering aspects of preparation, instruction, and consequences. Throughout the manual, sample forms are included, as is a list of IEP information resources.

409. Guidelines for Public School Programs Serving Visually Handicapped Children.† Spungin, Susan Jay. New York: American Foundation for the Blind, Inc., 1978, 60p.

The document provides guidelines for the mainstreaming of visually handicapped students as mandated by Public Law 94-142 (the Education for All Handicapped Children Act). Section I deals with legislation (including regulations, the individualized education program, and due process), funding, population (both identification and assessment), program design (service delivery system and specifications), and personnel and program requirements (including management and qualifications). The Program section details organization, continuum of services (including teacher consultant, itinerant teacher, resource room, special class, and special school programs), early childhood programs, assessment for educational planning (including such areas as eye specialist's assessment), and teacher responsibilities (such as teacher/student ratios and caseload class size). Section III describes the following program supports: physical facilities, materials and equipment, ancillary services, and national/state/local resources. Appendixes include the National Society for the Prevention of Blindness's Vision Screening of Children.

410. Hints and Activities for Mainstreaming.† Metsker, Carol J.; King, Edith. Dansville, NY: Instructor Curriculum Materials, 1977, 48p.

The booklet gives background information on learning disabled, educable mentally retarded, physically handicapped, visually and hearing impaired children, and provides suggestions on incorporating them into regular classes. Described are activities such as interviews and role playing tasks designed to emphasize similarities among children. Specific hints and activity suggestions are broken down for two types of special children: those who have difficulty learning and those with physical limitations.

411. Individualizing Educational Materials for Special Children in the Mainstream.† Anderson, Robert M. et al. Baltimore, MD: University Park Press, 1978, 393p.

The book presents a framework for incorporating into education, both regular and special, a sequential program for the acquisition of a set of competencies related to the use of instructional materials. The book is divided into three major sections. The first section contains six chapters that examine the basic steps each educator must follow to ensure effective programing; the second contains five chapters with ideas and suggestions designed to further enhance the overall effectiveness of the model described in section 1; and the final section contains three chapters examining other sources to which a teacher may turn for assistance in providing individualized instructional programing for special children in the mainstream. Chapters include the following titles and authors: "Assessing Learner Characteristics" (V. Laycock); "Critical Dimensions of Instructional Materials" (Laycock); "Making the Match—Rationale for Selection" (Laycock); "Retrieving Appropriate Materials" (K. Oglesby, et al.); "Evaluating Materials" (R. Spinney, et al.); "Constructing and Adapting Materials" (S. Odle); "Adapting the Learning Environment for Hearing Impaired, Visually Impaired, and Physically Handicapped" (B. Greer and J. Allsop); "Supplementary Media Resources" (P. Walls, et al.); "Affective Concerns in the Utilization of Instructional Materials" (H. Rich); "Instructional Games" (J. Greer, et al.); "Educational Media and Materials—Selected Resources and References" (J. Anderson, et al.); "Models for Mainstreaming Special Children" (J. Schifani, et al.); and "Prototype Materials for Effective Mainstreaming" (R. Anderson, et al.).

412. Mainstreaming: A Practical Guide. Paul, James L. et al. Syracuse, NY: Syracuse University Press, 1977, 147p.

This book offers practical guidelines for planning and implementing mainstreaming at the local school level. Chapter I describes a process for planning which results in the individual school being organizationally and psychologically ready for mainstreaming. Chapter II examines the roles and responsibilities of students, parents, and the community in mainstreaming. Chapter III discusses the roles and responsibilities of central administrators and principals, regular classroom teachers, resource teachers, school psychologists, counselors and therapists relative to placement procedures, individualizing instruction, social adjustment, and parent consultation. Chapter IV describes the changes needed in inservice teacher education and discusses specific ways to implement these changes in training teachers. Chapter V focuses on preservice teacher education and analyzes the changes needed in curriculum, faculty and training procedures in schools of education. Chapter VI deals with implementing mainstreaming, including a discussion of principles of program development and implementation. Problems and issues involved in implementing mainstreaming at the local school level are also described and recommendations are made for improving that process.

413. Mainstreaming Guidebook for Vocational Educators: Teaching the Handicapped.† Dahl, Peter R. et al. Salt Lake City, UT: Olympus Publishing Co., 1978, 352p.

Designed for vocational educators, the guidebook provides information on mainstreaming handicapped children. Chapter 1 discusses the rationale for and implementation of mainstreaming. The second chapter is concerned with developing positive staff and student attitudes toward mainstreaming. Chapter 3 describes desirable architectural features of a vocational facility to make it more useable for the handicapped. The fourth chapter presents models for assessing handicapped students and shows how to use assessment results to prepare an individualized instructional plan for handicapped students. Chapter 5 explores how to modify curriculum and teaching methods so that handicapped students can be taught in the same classrooms with nonhandicapped peers. The sixth chapter lists a variety of problems that might arise in the use of tools and equipment and demonstrates how these problems can be overcome with equipment modification or the use of aids and devices. Chapter 7 explains how handicapped graduates can be placed in jobs. The final chapter provides a summary of the book. A brief description of four handicapping conditions, a list of agencies and organizations serving the handicapped, and a suggested guideline model for use in developing and reviewing individualized educational programs are appended.

414. Mainstreaming Handicapped Students: A Guide for the Classroom Teacher.† Turnbull, Ann P.; Schulz, Jane B. Rockleigh, NJ: Allyn and Bacon, Inc., 1979, 386p.

Ten chapters in the text review practices and principles for the regular class teacher of mainstreamed handicapped children. The first chapter considers educational characteristics of cognitive, physical, communicative, sensory, and emotional/behavioral disadvantages. The background, legislative requirements, and purposes of mainstreaming are discussed. Aspects of developing and implementing an individualized educational program are detailed in two separate chapters. The final six chapters provide practical information and suggestions on teaching language arts (listening, speaking, writing and reading), arithmetic, science, social studies, physical education, music, and art. Also described are procedures for changing behavior and enhancing social integration. Among six appendixes are a learning style questionnaire and a developmental scale for determining language levels.

415. Mainstreaming Language Arts and Social Studies: Special Ideas and Activities for the Whole Class. Adams, Anne H. et al. Santa Monica, CA: Goodyear Publishing Co., 1977, 107p.

This book has thirty-six weeks' worth of activities that straddle the range of interests and abilities in mainstreamed classrooms. For each content area, 180 daily lesson plans—each with objectives, teacher preparations, and activities—are grouped under 36 survival-centered themes, such as following printed directions, detecting facts and opinions, comparing different foods, and deemphasizing sex- role stereotypes. None of the lessons require special equipment.

416. Mainstreaming Science and Mathematics: Special Ideas and Activities for the Whole Class. Coble, Charles R. et al. Santa Monica, CA: Goodyear Publishing Co., 1977, 123p.

Designed for the classroom teacher, this book presents 180 daily lesson plans each in science and mathematics—all designed to straddle the range of interests and abilities in mainstreamed classrooms. Lessons are grouped into 36 weekly themes such as describing textures, odors, and sounds of objects; investigating gravity; communicating with numbers; and using charge accounts. Each lesson includes objectives, teacher preparation, and learning activities.

417. Mainstreaming the Hearing Impaired Child: An Educational Alternative. Orlansky, Janice Zatsman. Austin, TX: Learning Concepts, 1977, 111p.

This book uses a cartoon format to introduce classroom teachers to hearing handicaps and the implications of placing hearing impaired pupils in the regular classroom. Definitions, classroom techniques, and positive attitudes are discussed.

418. Mainstreaming the Visually Impaired Child: Blind and Partially Sighted Students in the Regular Classroom. Orlansky, Michael D. Boston, MA: Teaching Resources, 1977, 121p.

Written in cartoon format, this guide discusses types of visual impairments; how the regular class teacher can help (attitudes, social growth, mobility, classroom arrangement, braille, approaches to teaching); and curriculum areas.

419. Mainstreaming with Special Emphasis on the Educable Mentally Retarded. Watson, Marjorie. Washington, DC: National Education Association, 1977, 80p.

Intended for regular class teachers and administrators, this book begins with a general review of the advantages and disadvantages of mainstreaming. The author then considers the causes and characteristics of mental retardation; educational goals; mainstreaming versus special classes; regular class techniques; possible problems for the teacher; and structure, content, and evaluation of the elementary school program. Appendixes include excerpts from P.L. 94-142 and a selected annotated bibliography on mainstreaming.

420. The Physically Handicapped Child: Facilitating Regular Classroom Adjustment. Hanna, Rick L.; Graff, Donald L. Austin, TX: Learning Concepts, 1977, 122p.

Using a cartoon format, this book provides the regular class teacher with definitions of physical handicaps and a discussion of architectural, medical, personal, and educational considerations for mainstreaming. An architectural accessibility compliance checklist is appended.

421. A Selected Annotated Bibliography on PL 94-142: Practical Programs for the Classroom, No. 13 in the Series of Bibliographies on Educational Topics (BETS). Washington, DC: ERIC Clearinghouse on Teacher Education, 1980.

As a result of new legislation (P.L. 94-142), all handicapped children are entitled to education in a regular classroom setting. This compilation of over 140 annotated citations will help teachers, administrators, and parents to cope with this new classroom situation. As the title suggests, the bibliography focuses on those documents and journal articles in the ERIC databases that present techniques for ''mainstreaming'' handicapped students.

422. Supporting Visually Impaired Students in the Mainstream. Martin, Glenda J.; Hoben, Mollie. Reston, VA: Council for Exceptional Children, Publication Sales Unit, 1977, 73p.

The handbook on the successful mainstreaming of visually impaired students provides a description of four mainstreaming programs, a discussion of principles and practices derived from the four programs, and practical suggestions for classroom teachers who will have a visually impaired student for the first time. Part I examines four successful mainstream programs, identifies the elements of success, and describes the interrelated roles and responsibilities of regular and special educators. Part II presents—in question and answer format—one perspective on how the general concepts and attitudes upon which successful mainstream programs are built become translated into the daily activities and responses of the educators in such areas as mobility, curriculum content, and peer relationships. Considered in Part III are an expanded concept of support (which includes development of daily living skills and personal independence) for visually impaired children in the mainstream, descriptions of how several school districts are responding to the expanded concept challenge, and the implications of meeting the expanded concept challenge.

423. Teaching Physically Handicapped Children: Methods and Materials. Love, Harold D. Springfield, IL: Charles C Thomas, 1978, 165p.

Although most physically handicapped children will be educated in the regular classroom, it is the author's contention that special methods and materials should be employed to aid these students. The concept of methods and materials is defined to encompass those theoretical and empirical functions that contribute to the education of the child. As such, it treats the behavior of orthopedically impaired children, children having special health problems and children with sensory defects, and describes approaches to evaluation, description, and education.

Emphasis in this volume is placed on the educational and psychological evaluation of the child, and the planning of an educational program aimed ultimately at vocational placement.

The book initially provides an historical overview of the handicapped child. Succeeding chapters discuss testing procedures, teaching language arts and math to orthopedically handicapped children, methods in teaching cerebral palsied children, architectural barriers in the school, and the school's responsibility for vocational placement of the child.

Special chapters deal with short-term educational goals for children having seriously handicapping problems and how parental attitudes affect the adjustment and achievements of handicapped children.

424. Teaching Students with Behavior Disorders: Techniques for Classroom Instruction.† Gallagher, Patricia A. Denver, CO: Love Publishing Co., 1979, 300p.

The book describes the structured approach, an educational intervention strategy for use in teaching behaviorally disordered students who are experiencing social and academic failures. Preacademic year planning for the teacher is discussed, beginning with the teacher's employment interview and covering ordering classroom materials and arranging the classroom environment. Aspects of educational diagnosis covered include diagnostic conference organization, academic subjects and skills assessment, assessment of environmental conditions, assessment of teaching techniques, assessment of student interests, and ongoing diagnosis. The selection and adaptation of educational materials is reviewed, along with the making of curriculum materials, and the creating of learning centers. Programing guidelines, teacher designed programs, and learning principles relevant to programing are examined. Techniques of behavior modification are described, and its use as a diagnostic tool is discussed, along with reinforcement and cautions in behavior modification. A basic behavior modification plan for intervention is presented. Some guidelines for scheduling are offered, along with daily scheduling techniques. Maintenance (the continuance and enrichment of the special class environment) and phasing out (the procedure by which special class students are gradually integrated into the mainstream of regular school activities) are also covered, including using the substitute teacher to continue the structured approach during the teacher's absence, and communicating with the parents to establish cooperative home-school relationships to expand the special environment. Appendixes, found at the ends of chapters, provide supplementary information of a practical nature to aid the teacher in carrying out the procedures suggested within those chapters.

Subject Index

Documents discussing specific disabilities or specific school subjects are indexed under the appropriate headings, except in cases where a single document discusses three or more different disabilities or school subjects. For these materials, see the headings "Various Handicaps" and "Various Subjects."

Academic Achievement, 56, 90, 220, 224, 236, 242, 247, 264, 282, 284, 294, 300, 303
Administrator Attitudes, 48, 49, 50, 67, 102, 104, 213, 308
Administrator Guides, 20, 30, 129, 169–69, 183, 195, 241, 245, 251, 259, 340, 346, 354, 362, 364–65, 379–80, 392, 396–97, 400, 409, 412
Administrator Role, 24, 29, 88, 119, 135–37, 140, 142, 147, 150, 182, 292, 321, 350, 401, 412
Ancillary Services, 183, 186, 188, 198, 219, 229, 235–36, 243, 248, 265, 355, 397
Architectural Accessibility, 5, 15, 18, 46, 52, 66, 95, 185, 187, 192, 227, 235, 244, 259, 336, 339–40, 362, 413, 420
Attitudes of the Handicapped, 58, 101, 130
Audiovisual Aids, 164, 173, 177, 179
Aurally Handicapped, 155, 188, 198, 227, 236, 254, 278, 281, 300, 304, 309, 344, 369, 382, 387, 417
Autism, 204, 208, 217, 312
Behavior Disorders, 145, 295, 343, 350, 380–81, 424
Behavior Modification, 92, 208, 224, 267–68, 393, 424

Bibliographies, 153, 173, 314, 319, 326, 353, 359, 363, 398, 401, 419, 421
Blind. *See* Visually Handicapped.
Building Design, 5, 192, 259, 332, 340, 352, 395, 409. *See also* Architectural Accessibility.

Changing Attitudes, 62, 74, 75, 80, 90, 94, 98, 99, 107, 125, 127, 148, 240, 413
Class Size, 44, 61, 63
Classroom Teachers. *See* Regular Class Teachers.
Classroom Techniques, 86, 158, 301, 304, 311, 322, 324, 327–29, 333, 343–45, 348, 356, 359, 375, 377, 403, 406–07, 410, 417–18, 420–21
Collective Bargaining, 55, 61, 207
Communicatively Handicapped. *See* Language Handicapped.
Community Agencies, 108, 219
Competency Based Education, 209, 404
Competition, 1
Cooperative Planning, 123, 127–29, 134–35, 141, 143, 151, 161–62, 172, 186, 198, 217, 219, 223, 243, 256–57, 262, 265, 315, 318, 321, 351, 396, 412
Costs, 32, 189–90, 193, 276, 284
Counseling Services, 160, 316, 397
Counselor Role, 108–111, 116, 132, 141, 315–17, 351, 355
Court Litigation, 2, 4, 7, 13, 17, 52, 54, 112, 114, 150, 203, 277, 291
Curriculum Development, 87, 100, 249, 313, 339, 404–05, 411

Deaf. *See* Aurally Handicapped.
Decision Making, 39, 112, 114, 136, 144, 146, 269, 272–73, 275, 278, 281, 283, 287, 289, 295–97, 301–4, 307–8, 346

Directories, 174, 181, 323, 330, 336, 353
Discipline, 34, 83, 333, 343
Due Process, 2, 3, 13, 21, 27, 35, 36, 150, 171, 292, 354

Educable Mentally Handicapped, 80, 89, 92, 105, 204, 242, 252, 271, 274, 285, 308, 392–93, 419
Elementary Education, 10, 12, 46, 48, 49, 73, 79, 80, 99, 100, 103, 106, 111, 126, 132, 157, 179, 204, 211, 214, 220, 247, 252, 257, 264, 315–17, 325, 341, 350, 356
Emotionally Disturbed, 34, 79, 145, 243, 246, 268, 288, 298, 307, 343, 350, 367, 377, 380–81, 424
Ethics, 1, 8, 14, 398
Exemplary Practices. *See* Success Factors.

Foreign Countries, 26, 37, 349
Funding, 33, 65, 190, 258, 264, 397

Government Role, 4, 7, 19

Hard of Hearing. *See* Aurally Handicapped.
Health Services, 133, 332, 368
Higher Education, 18, 32, 42, 43, 66, 95, 108, 115, 130, 155, 183, 185–86, 188, 235–36, 244, 266, 336, 352, 355, 362
Historical Reviews, 4, 7, 8, 19, 25, 29, 240

Individual Differences, 1, 76, 77, 87, 298
Individual Education Plans (IEPs), 45, 51, 57, 59, 69, 72, 111, 119, 124, 129, 134, 138, 152, 156, 161–62, 166–67, 178, 199–200, 207, 211, 313, 318, 337, 351, 357, 358, 361, 387–91, 408, 414

Individualized Instruction, 118, 214, 218, 247, 260, 277, 310

Inservice Education. *See* Training Chapter.

Instructional Materials, 100, 153, 157–58, 160, 162–64, 166–68, 171, 173–81, 224, 314, 322, 326, 329–30, 334, 337, 339, 341–42, 347, 353, 358, 387–91, 411

Interpersonal Competence, 81, 105, 338, 399, 424

Language Arts, 325, 415

Language Handicapped, 265, 325, 360, 373, 383, 388, 403

Learning Disabilities, 89, 99, 175, 189, 201, 210, 225, 237, 245, 260, 273, 280, 282, 284, 287, 294–95, 310, 317, 338, 347, 370, 384, 389, 392–94, 402

Least Restrictive Environment, 2, 3, 6, 19, 36, 119, 202, 249–50, 406

Legal Responsibility, 15–19, 21, 23, 28, 52, 54, 67, 114, 124, 171, 354, 365

Mainstreaming—Advantages and Disadvantages, 10, 22, 25, 34, 37, 53, 61, 69, 78, 96, 122, 184, 202, 206, 210–11, 213, 222, 226, 233–34, 253–54, 267, 280, 282, 284–86, 288, 291, 293–94, 298, 300, 305–6, 399, 419

Mathematics, 394, 416

Mentally Handicapped, 205, 212, 269, 291, 371, 378, 405. *See also* Educable Mentally Handicapped and Trainable Mentally Handicapped.

Mentally Retarded, 11, 305

Mildly Handicapped, 10, 50, 73, 107, 152, 165, 221, 247, 251, 272, 301

Minority Groups, 17, 25, 124, 233, 261

Models, 159, 165, 170, 172, 187, 192, 194–98, 201, 218–19, 232, 235–36, 240, 244, 246, 248–51, 253, 260, 263–64, 267, 311, 331, 349, 380, 392

Multiply Handicapped, 332

Needs Assessment, 113, 170, 185, 223, 244, 259, 379

Nonhandicapped Peers, 94, 103, 148, 204–5, 211, 229, 233, 237

Orthopedically Handicapped. *See* Physically Handicapped.

PL 94-142. *See* Provisions of PL 94-142.

Paraprofessional School Personnel, 155, 158, 228

Parent Attitudes, 24, 58, 72, 75, 101, 234, 238, 271, 297, 299–300, 305

Parent Role, 2, 22, 30, 33, 39, 129, 134, 166–67, 178, 228, 232, 292, 396

Parents, 88, 128, 156

Peer Acceptance, 23, 64, 75, 77, 80, 81, 85–87, 91, 94–96, 100, 101, 103, 141, 148, 179, 242, 253, 257, 267, 291, 304, 317, 320, 322, 334–35, 338, 341–42, 410

Physical Education, 120, 199, 237, 359, 375, 399

Physically Handicapped, 103, 276, 283, 318, 328, 339, 355, 368, 372, 375, 395, 420, 423

Preschool Programs, 16, 56, 64, 81, 201, 228, 232, 253, 267, 279, 288, 330, 334, 349, 358, 367–74

Principals, 88, 102, 104, 119, 135–37, 140, 142, 146–47, 169, 292, 306, 321, 365

Private Schools, 215, 306

Program Evaluation, 40, 41, 44, 47, 51, 56, 57, 59, 60, 65, 70, 71, 72, 84, 150, 170, 194–96, 216, 238, 244, 259, 261, 264

Provisions of PL 94-142, 3, 6, 12, 15, 19, 20, 21, 27, 31, 35, 36, 47, 52, 60, 67, 114, 166, 178, 229, 253

Provisions of Section 504, 5, 15, 18, 30, 52, 352, 362. *See also* Architectural Accessibility.

Psychologists, 138–39, 148

Reading, 313, 319, 394

Records (Forms), 23, 27, 31, 131, 263, 281, 351, 354, 357, 361, 382–86, 396, 408

Regular Class Teachers, 34, 48, 49, 50, 63, 68, 73, 79, 89, 97–99, 104, 106, 117, 121, 123, 126–27, 143, 157, 165, 175, 177, 422

Research Reviews, 24, 64, 75, 81, 84, 90, 92, 169, 250, 255, 319, 359

Resource Guides, 27, 31, 161, 163–64, 167, 173–74, 177, 181, 265, 323, 330, 336–37, 349, 352–53, 355, 357, 361, 366–374, 379, 382–86, 409, 411

Resource Rooms, 189, 196, 223, 245, 248, 251, 263, 284, 338

Resource Teachers, 106, 196, 201, 218, 225–26, 239, 257, 381

School Nurses, 133

School Social Workers, 151

Science, 220, 324, 339, 395, 416

Secondary Education, 110, 147, 191, 205, 209, 218, 221, 238, 242, 245, 254, 263, 285, 380–81, 392–93, 402, 404

Section 504. *See* Provisions of Section 504.

Self Concept, 91, 286, 300, 326

Severely Handicapped, 182, 270, 275, 290, 296, 299, 346, 358, 406

Social Maturity, 92

Social Studies, 214, 415

Special Class Teachers, 63

Special Classes, 101, 189, 274, 282, 284, 291, 300, 307

Special Education Teachers, 49, 50, 68, 104, 123, 127, 131, 143, 145, 225, 422

Special Schools, 190, 197–98, 212, 243, 256, 262, 293, 299

Speech Handicapped. *See* Language Handicapped.

Spina Bifida, 328

State Officials, 36, 40, 47, 67, 118

State Plans, 62, 65, 70, 72, 133, 178, 209, 258, 306

Student Characteristics, 92, 254, 276, 281, 283, 303, 309, 312, 316, 328, 345, 348, 356, 366–74, 376–78, 394, 402–03, 406–07, 414, 417–20, 423

Student Motivation, 234, 312

Student Placement, 3, 6, 9, 11, 39, 76, 79, 252, 292, 346

Success Factors, 9, 64, 96, 135, 147, 206, 213, 217, 221, 230–31, 241, 252, 254, 281, 331, 360, 364, 422

Teacher Aides. *See* Paraprofessional School Personnel.

Teacher Attitudes, 34, 38, 44, 48, 49, 50, 51, 55, 62, 63, 68, 69, 71, 73, 74, 75, 79, 82, 83–85, 89, 90, 93, 96–99, 104–107, 141, 223, 225, 231, 273–74, 297, 299, 307–08

Teacher Centers, 154

Teacher Education (Preservice), 14, 42, 43, 78, 125, 149, 239, 266

Teacher Role, 9, 21, 22, 61, 84–86, 115, 117, 122, 124, 131, 144–45, 180, 246, 279, 289, 302, 357, 364, 398, 412, 422

Teaching Guides, 310–11, 319, 324–
    25, 327, 329–30, 335, 342, 344,
    347–49, 356, 360, 366–378,
    381, 387–91, 393–95, 398–99,
    402–03, 405–08, 410–11, 413,
    414–421, 423–24
Teaching Skills, 113, 117–18,
    120–21, 126, 128, 149, 175,
    203, 221, 245
Testing, 53, 109, 139, 209, 261, 378,
    394, 405, 423
Tests, 330, 337, 366, 381–86
Trainable Mentally Handicapped,
    222, 237–38, 270–71, 275, 290,
    385, 390
Transition Plans (for Students), 197,
    208, 217, 262, 302, 317, 335,
    346, 424
Tutoring, 191, 204–05

Various Handicaps (specifically dis-
    cusses 3 or more different dis-
    abilities), 51, 58, 59, 91, 97,
    104, 176, 179–80, 192–93, 220,
    235, 267, 316, 323–24, 326,
    329, 334, 342, 352, 356, 365,
    395, 397, 399, 407, 410–11,
    413–14
Various Subjects (specifically dis-
    cusses 3 or more school subject
    areas), 175, 310, 347, 360, 381,
    404, 414, 418, 423
Visually Handicapped, 219, 293,
    341, 345, 348, 374, 376, 386,
    391, 409, 418, 422
Vocational Education, 58, 74, 163,
    176, 203, 230–31, 250, 255,
    262, 366, 379, 397, 400, 413
Volunteers. *See* Paraprofessional
    School Personnel.